CAST-IRON
A Photographic Survey

ARCHITECTURE IN NEW YORK

Text by MARGOT GAYLE   Photographs by EDMUND V. GILLON, JR.

Dover Publications, Inc., New York

Published in Canada by General Publishing Company, Ltd., 30 Lesmill Road, Don Mills, Toronto, Ontario.
Published in the United Kingdom by Constable and Company, Ltd., 10 Orange Street, London WC 2.

Cast-Iron Architecture in New York is a new work, first published by Dover Publications, Inc., in 1974.

International Standard Book Number: 0-486-22980-7
Library of Congress Catalog Card Number: 74-78493

Manufactured in the United States of America
Dover Publications, Inc.
180 Varick Street
New York, N. Y. 10014

INTRODUCTION

What Is
a Cast-Iron Building?

Many people have been walking past cast-iron buildings all their lives without realizing it. This is not surprising, since the original owners and builders of iron structures intended their buildings to look like stone. Especially in the early days of iron architecture during the pre-Civil War period, builders faithfully copied popular Renaissance stone designs, and then painted the buildings in typical light stone colors. Every effort was made to deceive the beholder into thinking the iron fronts were made of stone.

The iron buildings we are talking about are commercial structures in old downtown areas of Manhattan, where buildings line the streets, side by side, usually having only one facade exposed, this facade being the part made of iron. Where such a building is on a corner site, the front facing on the principal thoroughfare is of iron, and usually the second side as well (361 Broadway, p. 130, 488 Broadway, p. 142)—but not always, for economy often dictated that the side-street facade be of brick (55 White St., p. 28, 500 Broome, p. 56).

The greatest concentration of iron-front buildings is in the SoHo area (discussed below), but many others stand alone on various city blocks south of 29th St. At the northern outpost of 29th and Broadway stands the great ghost of the 1869 Gilsey Hotel (p. 166). Farther up Manhattan one can find only Peck and Hill's store on

East 34th St. and such part-iron fronts as the Far Gallery at 746 Madison Avenue and the grand two-story arch with filigree and side columns that gives such character to the Scribner Building by Ernest Flagg at 597 Fifth Avenue. It was cast in the vast Cornell Foundry.

Customarily the iron-front buildings are four to six stories tall, this being the greatest number of stories practical before passenger elevators came into general use. The few iron-front buildings that are appreciably taller are late examples, or have had stories added. One such structure is the 10-story Bennett Building at 93 Nassau St. (p. 5). Built in 1872 as an important office building for an important New Yorker, James Gordon Bennett, 93 Nassau contained an elevator from the outset. Even in this instance, the upper four floors were added several years later. In addition, the Bennett Building is one of the few with three sides of iron.

Behind the average iron-front facade is a very conventional internal structure with brick bearing-walls at side and rear, with wooden beams and joists and with wooden floors. When cast iron occurs inside iron-front buildings it is almost always in the form of slender columns supporting the floors. Not only do these slender though strong uprights permit a very open interior and an unprecedented amount of usable floor space; they are often extremely handsome. Usually painted white, they may be fluted and may have rich Corinthian capitals picked out with touches of gold paint. Some stand as tall as 16 or 18 feet, especially in buildings designed for elegant retail stores (old Arnold Constable's, p. 164). Iron appears constantly in stair elements—treads, railings, often the entire staircase —for safety against fire. And occasionally in the larger iron buildings we find a primitive iron framing which foretells today's steel skyscrapers.

Ascertaining whether or not a given building has a front all or partly of cast iron becomes easy after a little practice. The first thing to determine is whether the surface is painted. Sometimes stone has been painted, but wood and iron always are. Then, iron feels cooler to the touch then wood. Some people administer a sharp rap with a coin and expect to detect a metallic sound, but that is hard to hear. Of course, any rust is a dead giveaway; it is useful to step back and look over the front of the building searching for rusty spots. Next, scan the design for places where small decorative parts have become loose, are askew or are missing altogether. Stone will weather away gradually, so that carved stone details lose their crisp edges, but cast iron stays crisp except for layers of paint. The incontrovertible test is the magnet test; real cast-iron buffs always carry pocket magnets.

At the close of the 19th century many, many more iron-front buildings than exist today stood along the downtown streets of Manhattan and Brooklyn. Brooklyn now has only two or three, but (even not counting buildings with iron on the ground floor only) Manhattan has between 250 and 300 iron-front buildings. This is more than any other city has. A large proportion of the New York cast-iron buildings are represented in this book, all of the more significant and familiar ones and many of those less well known.

The 19th-Century Cast-Iron Streetscape; Cast-Iron Construction

Iron-front stores, office buildings, warehouses and hotels hummed with commercial activity in their heyday and were objects of great pride to their owners. They formed an extremely attractive part of the City's streetscape. Most were elaborate in design, some positively florid by today's aesthetic standards. They were well kept and were painted frequently. Gleaming with nearly white paint, their many large windows sparkling, and with striped awnings shading the sidewalks, they were a breathtaking contrast to the understated Federal and Greek Revival red brick buildings with small multipaned windows that formed the backdrop of the earlier city.

In the age of the gas jet, and later, of the naked incandescent light bulb, welcome daylight could pour into the iron buildings—both for merchandise display in ground-floor stores and for manufacturing, handling orders and bookkeeping on the upper floors. Big windows were made possible because iron is so strong in compression, that is, under downward pressure. A few slender columns could support an entire facade.

Often big retail establishments were constructed with several floors of galleries around a central court with a glass and iron skylight overhead. Wanamaker's and Altman's (p. 105) were like this and reminded New Yorkers of Paris emporiums, such as the Bon Marché with its elaborate skylights engineered by A. Gustave Eiffel of Eiffel Tower renown.

The use of iron also opened up new interior space, the tall, thin supporting columns permitting high ceil-

Figure 1. Interior view of the New York Crystal Palace. From *The World of Science, Art and Industry Illustrated, 1873*. Courtesy New York State Historical Association, Cooperstown.

ings and extensive open floor areas. A whole new and dramatic concept of open space was made possible by the flexible new materials, iron and glass, as seen in old prints of the New York Crystal Palace (Fig. 1), built in 1853 on what is now Bryant Park, and in photographs of R. G. Hatfield's train shed arching over the tracks at the rear of the first Grand Central Station on 42nd St., designed by John B. Snook.

Merchants and wholesalers, the best customers for iron-front buildings, also responded to another advantage of cast-iron architecture—the speed and economy with which it could be constructed. The many sections of an iron facade were cast at the foundry in molds, then finished and the smaller parts assembled and bolted together. Prior to delivery the entire front was laid out on the floor of the foundry's fitting room. All parts were laid in place, numbered and tested for fit, after which a coat of protective paint was put on. At the construction site, the prefabricated parts were permanently assembled and bolted together, one story above another, the entire facade being anchored to the side walls of the building. This was prefabrication of a high order, a valuable addition to American construction technology at the very time that great economic and geographic expansion called for rapid construction of buildings.

Prefabricated iron parts could be shipped long distances by railroad or boat almost as readily as they could be tranported across town by horse-drawn drays. Thus, buildings fabricated in New York foundries rose not only on local streets, but also in distant towns and cities. To this day iron architecture made in New York can be seen in Halifax, Milwaukee, Savannah and San Francisco, not to mention such upstate New York communities as Rochester and Cooperstown.

Yet another aspect of cast iron that held enormous appeal for Victorian-era businessmen was the elegance that could be achieved. Virtually every architectural style was within reach. None was too bold or too delicate to be reproduced in iron, no decoration too intricate. Any desired shape could be recreated so long as the initial patterns could be carved, and then pressed into damp sand to form sand molds into which molten metal could flow. Since antiquity statues and architectural ornament had been made in bronze; now in the 19th century they were being turned out in quantity in the far cheaper medium of iron.

For beautiful castings on existing buildings in New York City, look at the columns of 361 Broadway (p. 130), the identical Medusa-face keystones of 260 Canal and 75 Murray Sts., (pp. 32 and 8) and the ivy-twined colonnettes of the old Stern's store on West 23rd St. (p. 118). Then, for overall precision casting, study the two facades of the Haughwout Building (p. 142). Craftsmanship of a high standard must have prevailed in the foundries which produced these examples and the detailing on many of New York's iron fronts.

Changing Fashions in Cast-Iron Exteriors

The first iron-front design was based on a very simple post-and-lintel concept with a relatively small amount of decoration. It was executed by inventor-designer-engineer James Bogardus in the late 1840s on three sites: Dr. John Milhau's pharmacy at 183 Broadway, Edgar Laing's row of five stores on Washington St. and Bogardus's own factory on Centre St. None is standing now. Iron was cast in the same molds for all three. The important career of the pioneer Bogardus is discussed below in the section "Great Names in Cast-Iron Architecture."

Soon the Italianate style took over in cast iron, as it already had in masonry, both for commercial buildings and for the proliferating rows of town houses. The Renaissance-style Italian palazzo, a spacious, rectangular building of several stories, quite suited to a functional commercial structure, had been introduced into England by Sir Charles Barry in his 1830 Travellers' Club, according to Henry-Russell Hitchcock. By 1839 a monograph concerning it had been published. Perhaps this is what aroused interest in New York and led the prominent merchant A. T. Stewart to have his 1845 marble store based on the palazzo ideal. Now known as the Sun Building, this edifice still stands at 280 Broadway, near City Hall. It is threatened with demolition by the City, which should preserve it as a landmark. Its grandiose scale and elegant design set a style that was embraced heartily by the creators of cast-iron architecture.

Stewart's marble store antedates the City's first iron building by only three years. Only 17 years after his first store was begun, Stewart had his second, uptown, store done as a block-square palazzo in cast iron (see pp. 160 and 161). Iron founder John B. Cornell told of standing alongside Stewart as they admired his big new

1862 iron store with its white-painted Italianate arches piled tier on tier and of Stewart's exclaming: "It is like puff on puff of white clouds." Now that this marvel is gone, the great remaining palazzo archetype in iron is the 1856 Haughwout Building (p. 142). Other examples can be seen at 427 Broadway (p. 135) and 260 Canal St. at Lafayette (p. 32). All of these stand on corners and have two facades of iron.

The palace styles of Venice were reflected in many New York iron fronts which stood shoulder to shoulder along streets just as the Venetian palaces stand along the canals. Although now sandwiched between 20th-century buildings, 75 Murray St. (p. 8) is the perfect example.

In this first Italianate phase the round-headed window prevailed. It could be produced so readily in the medium of iron! Especially favored was a window motif derived from the Roman Colosseum or from Sansovino's Library in Venice. It was comprised of an arch springing from small columns, flanked by larger columns supporting an entablature, which gave a strong horizontal line at each story. Scarcely any wall surfaces were left unbroken, and decorated "keystones" and balustrades enriched the facades. The street scene took on a thoroughly ornate mien.

As the century progressed, the High Victorian Italianate brought in taller segmental-arched windows with the arches held on stilts or impost blocks. Often the impost block was accented by a bracket supporting the cornice above it. The overhanging roof cornices, now held by elaborate over-scaled brackets, often rose in central pediments which bore the date of the building or the name of the owner.

The prolific New York architect Griffith Thomas, who designed so many buildings in cast iron, stripped this model down for a simpler facade with deep window reveals, flat-topped and slightly arched at the corners. Bold columns between these windows increased the surface modeling and hence the play of light and shadow, giving a very forthright effect which can be readily recognized as Thomas'. His warehouses and stores, several of which appear in this book, are characterized by the repetition across the surface of the building of identical modules, permitting mass production of the iron components.

The Victorian client undoubtedly liked the opulent and ever-so-solid look of the columned stories piled one on the other, complemented by as much orna-mental detail as he chose. In stone, shaped and carved like this, perhaps with fluted columns and Corinthian capitals, such a structure would have cost a princely sum. In cast iron it was within his means.

France was the source of the favorite style of the seventies. The Second Empire mode changed Paris and found so many admirers here that it also changed New York for a while. Architects and clients alike must have been pleased with the piling of masses and the mansard roofs, which broke the skyline with peaks and domes topped with lacy iron cresting. Although such Second Empire monuments in masonry as the Booth Theatre and the Masonic Hall (which faced each other on West 23rd St.) are gone, three stellar examples in cast iron are still to be seen. These are the iron facade of the old Arnold Constable's at Fifth Avenue and 19th St. with its high mansard roof (p. 164); the Gilsey Hotel, with a clock in its roof (p. 166); and the comparatively understated front with mansard roof at One Bond St. (p. 88).

Toward the end of the 19th century a repose descends upon the design in iron-front buildings. There is a new restraint in the Ehrich Brothers' store on Sixth Avenue (p. 112), in Ludwig's Clothing Store extension on West 14th St. (p. 104) and in McCutcheon's Linen Store and the new 1905 iron and pressed-metal facade of Best's Lilliputian Bazaar (McCutcheon's and Best's are both on West 23rd St., pp. 120 and 117), while the 1901 iron front at 550 Broadway (p. 146) is nearly Bauhaus in style.

The Use of Cast Iron in Alterations

In the small amount of 20th-century writing on cast-iron architecture, there is no recognition of one frequent use of the 19th-century iron fronts. This was a cosmetic use: iron fronts were quite often put onto existing old buildings as a way of giving them an up-to-date appearance. Present-day materials employed for such a purpose include the ubiquitous aluminum siding, fake brick, sheets of shiny or colored enameled metal, laminated wood, even mirrored surfaces. But a freshly painted cast-iron front certainly added a stylish look in its day that none of these can in ours.

The professional architectural literature of the 1860s and 1870s in which the discussions of iron as a building material are found, has little if anything to say of this aspect of iron architecture. James Bogardus himself seems not to have acclaimed it as an advantage of building in iron when he wrote his celebrated 1856 promotional pamphlet. Yet a study of the old records discloses that Bogardus' very first sale of an iron front may well have been for just such a use. He sold it to a famous pharmacist, Dr. John Milhau, son of high-born French refugees from the 1793 San Domingo revolution. Milhau established his pharmacy in 1830 in a four-story building at 183 Broadway. He was a leader and an innovator. He established the N. Y. College of Pharmacy, helped form the American Pharmaceutical Association, and lobbied a law through Congress to prevent adulterated drugs from being imported. When he sought to improve his Broadway building, which was less than 20 feet wide, he had it raised one story in 1848 and got Bogardus to sell him the prefabricated parts for an iron front to be put over its facade. As Bogardus is said to have had the parts ready-cast to begin erection of his all-iron factory on Duane St., he gladly diverted enough modules to provide the Milhau iron front, which according to Moses King, writing in 1892, "was completed in the astonishingly short space of three days."

Sometimes an iron front would be put over an old commercial structure to spruce up its image for a business already occupying it. Such was the case with Dr. Milhau's drugstore, and such was the case with James A. Roosevelt's glass and mirror-importing firm on Maiden Lane. In June of 1869, he and his father Cornelius V. S. Roosevelt had expanded their store by purchasing the building next door. After Cornelius' death his son had a very tasteful iron front applied onto the street elevation of the two old brick buildings, joining them together. Also, with the help of architect James Wright, he had a stylish mansard roof added, providing a fourth story and unifying the design of the Roosevelt firm's "new" building (p. 4).

The story of 140–142 Pearl St. is a little more complicated (p. 1). In 1868 a well known firm of tea merchants purchased and occupied 140 Pearl, and then decided to have its four-story brick facade covered with a fine new iron front. For this they employed architect Griffith Thomas, and the building bears his characteristic stamp—the broad flat-arched windows separated by solid half-round columns, the marked cornice at every floor, and the roof cornice carried on brackets. Seven years later, having purchased the old four-story brick

building at 142, previously occupied by the N. Y. Cotton Exchange, they called Thomas back. He was commissioned to put a matching iron front on 142 and to make both it and 140 one story higher. Demonstrating the versatility of iron as a material, he was able to use the same molds, matching the iron perfectly for the new facade.

An even more prevalent practice was the use of new iron fronts to convert old houses into commercial buildings. This happened again and again, as residential neighborhoods were preempted for business use. One of the earliest remaining examples of this use of an iron front appears at 171 Duane St. (p. 16), where an 1828 Federal house of some pretensions was enlarged to cover what had been its rear garden, and then received an iron front on the side facing Duane St. Park. This was done in 1859 and served to make a significant commercial building out of a three-story brick mansion.

At almost the same time a five-story iron front was being put over a brick building, the one-time residence and shop of silversmith Augustus Thomas at 63 Nassau St. (p. 2). We can well imagine that office space was much in demand so near the City's only post office and other commercial facilities. When Julian Gauton bought the brick structure in 1859, he at once erected additional stories and had the elaborate, if narrow, iron front put on it. Probably this front was fabricated by Bogardus, who seems to have employed certain of the molds used for two of his famous earlier buildings, the Baltimore Sun Building and the Harper and Brothers Building.

In this book are at least a half dozen other instances where the application of a new iron front entirely refurbished the facade of an existing building. Among these are Edith Wharton's girlhood home (p. 120), two houses transformed into Best's children's wear store (p. 117), and the two houses that look as if they were wearing Halloween hats (p. 114)—all on West 23rd St. Also there is merchant Robert McCurdy's house at 10 East 14th St., and Tiffany's former store at 550 Broadway, modernized for a new tenant with an iron front in 1901—undoubtedly the swan song of this type of use!

Great Names in Cast-Iron Architecture

Of the men most identified with cast-iron architecture, the name of James Bogardus comes first to mind.

Figure 2. The Bogardus factory at Duane and Center Sts., the nation's first all-iron building. Courtesy Museum of the City of New York.

Bogardus, born in 1800 in Catskill, N.Y., is an interesting American inventor who often promoted his inventions, and sometimes even manufactured them. He invented a dry gas-meter and a metal-cased "forever pointed" pencil. His device for an engraving machine for printing postage stamps was adopted by the English for their earliest stamps and brought him both income and international acclaim. His sugar-grinding eccentric mill design later earned him a good living. He produced it in his own factory, which he built in 1849 on the northeast corner of Centre and Duane Sts. (Fig. 2). It was the nation's first *all-iron* building.

Bogardus' prime interest for us lies in his patents for constructing prefabricated iron buildings of mass-produced parts, and in his activities as a contractor in erecting these earliest iron-front structures, which are recognized as an American architectural innovation. In 1848 he put up the first in the City, perhaps in the world. He seems never to have operated any sizable foundry, but to have contracted with various foundry-men and blacksmiths for production of building parts, and to have supervised their assembly. His personal taste is clearly reflected in the buildings with which he is identified (see page 21), although it is known that in

Figure 3. The cover of the D. D. Badger catalogue of 1865. The firm's office
building at 42 Duane St. is shown in the central view.

the case of the large two-sided 1851 iron building for the *Sun* newspaper in Baltimore, he worked with the architect Robert G. Hatfield. Some three years later he used the same molds, the wooden patterns for which had been stored for reuse, to make iron parts for architect John B. Corlies' famous Harper's Book Building, the Franklin Square site of which now lies beneath a high-rise apartment house alongside the Brooklyn Bridge. Bogardus used the molds again when he erected the Ahrenfeldt China Store on Murray St. that was not taken down until 1956. Apparently some of these molds were used for the portrait medallions on the fragile little iron front to be seen at 63 Nassau St. (p. 2).

Less than 10 years after putting up his 1848 building, Bogardus, together with an associate, John A. Thomson, wrote a pamphlet entitled *Cast-Iron Buildings: Their Construction and Advantages.* At the end of it he listed buildings which he had erected in Chicago, Philadelphia, Washington, Charleston, San Francisco and even Havana. He was really putting iron architecture on the map.

Bogardus was not only getting a lot of business, he was soon getting a lot of competition as well. Several small foundries which had been turning out stoves, garden furniture, fences, safes and decorative architectural elements such as balconies and stair rails, began to meet the demand for iron buildings. The chief New York City producers seem to have been James L. Jackson, J. B. & W. W. Cornell, Aetna Iron Works and Daniel Badger's Architectural Iron Works. There were many smaller foundries, too.

Badger, like the Cornells, eventually ran a huge foundry in lower Manhattan. His products are well-known to us because of the informative illustrated catalogue which he issued in 1865, the handsome cover of which is reproduced in Fig. 3. Few original copies exist, but a recent facsimile reprint has made it generally available.

Badger, born in 1806 on Badger's Island in New Hampshire, moved to Boston, where early city directories list him from 1830 to 1848 as a "blacksmith and whitesmith." According to his obituary in the New York *Times* of November 18, 1884, he experimented as early as 1842 with an iron store front on the ground floor of a building otherwise of masonry. It was the first in Boston, although the same sort of construction had been employed in New York City even earlier, as evi-

denced by an ad for a brick building "with heavy iron columns and lintel and shutters" that appeared in the New York *Commercial Advertiser* for August 15, 1836. Badger seems not to have envisioned the iron front of mass-produced interchangeable parts that Bogardus was working on.

But Badger did go on to great success after he came to New York in 1848. His first small foundry was at 42 Duane St., diagonally opposte Bogardus' conspicuous all-iron factory. Badger's first specialty was iron rolling shutters. He went on to fabricate elements for the increasingly popular iron fronts. By 1854 he had expanded to a site on East 14th St., between Avenues B and C, where his ever-growing great iron works turned out some of the most dramatic iron buildings this country has ever seem.

A young English architect on Badger's staff, George H. Johnson, created a great variety of modules. Sometimes Johnson put these together to make iron fronts for Badger clients, sometimes "name" architects used them to make their own creations. In other instances the architects prepared entirely new designs for which Badger, like other manufacturers, produced the iron components. The line is hard to draw. One Johnson module was such a favorite that in 1856 the architect John Kellum used it at 105 Chambers St. for W. H. Cary (p. 14), John B. Snook assembled it in 1858 for Henry Dolan at 620 Broadway (p. 150), and Daniel Badger used it for his own office building on the site of his original foundry at 42 Duane St. (the building shown in the center of Fig. 3). Meanwhile John Van Osdel had employed it in 1857 for attorney John Link's building in Chicago, which went down in the great fire of 1871. Then in 1860 Johnson used it to produce "The Iron Block" for James Martin in Milwaukee, which was designated an official city landmark in 1973. Finally it was used sometime before 1865 for both the Fireman's Insurance Company on Camp St. in New Orleans and for the Clay Building in Memphis. These buildings looked very different from one another, to judge from old prints of those now gone and photographs of those still standing, yet all were assembled from much the same basic parts.

The iron founder John B. Cornell made his mark on New York City after beginning as a manufacturer of iron safes in 1847. He and his brother William W. soon felt that their small foundry on Centre St. near Walker St. was too confining, and by 1859 they had built a foundry and fitting shops along the Hudson River at West 26th St. that could handle the big irons fronts for which they soon became famous. These included A. T. Stewart's 1862 iron palazzo (later Wanamaker's) and Tiffany's on Union Square, both now gone, as well as 503-511 Broadway and McCreery's Broadway store (p. 162) and such one-story shop fronts as those to be seen at 79 Leonard and 71 Franklin Sts. After William Cornell's death in 1870, John M. Cornell, son of John B., became his father's partner, so that we find the J. B. & J. M. Cornell trademark on such post-1870 buildings as Stern's store on 23rd St. (p. 118), 440 Broadway and 550 Broadway (p. 146). Father and son also cast the beautiful lacy balconies of the Chelsea Hotel on West 23rd St. (p. 181). During the Civil War the Cornell foundry made turrets for the Ericsson Monitors, and in later days turned to building elevated railroads. The firm is still in business, manufacturing rolling shutters.

In the 1860s New York and Brooklyn together had 41 iron founding establishments. They also had several real estate leaders who "believed in iron." In addition to his iron store, in 1870 A. T. Stewart built an iron residence hotel for working women at the northeast corner of Fourth Avenue and 32nd St. This large structure with its inner courtyard lasted till 1927. The use of iron supports made possible the sensational 11 by 7 foot plate-glass show windows on the ground floor of Stewart's 1848 marble store near City Hall. And to this day you can see at 18 Mercer St. one of the earliest commercial buildings erected in SoHo—an iron front which Badger did for Stewart in this then residential area. It is one of the most abused iron fronts in town.

Peter Gilsey was another developer who favored cast iron. His Gilsey Building, a large cast-iron office block, stood at the southwest corner of Cortlandt St. and Broadway looking impressive until 1905, when the Singer Tower soared up beside it. Not long after that it was demolished. Gilsey also built a big iron-front hotel and called it the Gilsey House. To it flocked the theatrical clientele of the neighborhood when the Rialto lay along Broadway between 23rd and 34th Sts. It is now a loft building (p. 166). The landowning Goelet family had several iron buildings, one of which stands at 809 Broadway.

Among the successful architects particularly identified with cast-iron buildings must be named the above-mentioned Griffith Thomas, John Kellum and John B. Snook, as well as Stephen B. Hatch, Henry Fernbach, the brothers David and John Jardine, and J. Morgan Slade. Several buildings by each of these men are pictured in this book. The much-admired Richard Morris Hunt twice tried his hand at designing in iron. His "Moorish style iron building" (Fig. 4) is gone, but 478 Broadway, which he built next to it for James Roosevelt, still stands, displaying much originality in handling the medium of iron (p. 140).

Cast-Iron Architecture in Other Cities

Where New York has a great existing heritage of iron architecture, other cities have demolished theirs through the years. Many iron fronts were lost when Independence Mall was carved out in Philadelphia. Ranges of iron fronts along the St. Louis waterfront were torn down to create the park in which the tall Saarinen steel arch is located. In Richmond, Virginia, the number of iron fronts along Main St. has been whittled to a very few by recent development. Chicago, which grew so fast that it favored prefabricated iron buildings before its great fire of 1870, and rebuilt in iron in many instances after the fire, has not a single entire iron front left. Baltimore is even now bulldozing iron-front buildings fabricated by its famous foundries as it proceeds with the clearance of its Inner Harbor Renewal Area. Soon it may have but one left, the Robins Paper Company's iron front at 310 West Pratt St., and it too seems doomed.

In some cities where an individual iron-front building has become a center of interest, it is being treasured and restored. For example, there is the iron-front grand opera house in Wilmington, Delaware, now being rehabilitated for the city's performing arts center. In Salt Lake City, the famed ZCMI department store's iron front is being given great care as the store is expanded behind it. In Seattle, an iron and glass pergola in Pioneer Square Park has been restored with newly cast duplicates replacing lost parts. A 1971 AIA Award went to Skidmore, Owings & Merrill for rebuilding an 1868 iron bank in Salem, Oregon (the ornate and enormously stylish Ladd and Bush U.S. National Bank), and expanding it with matching iron components salvaged in another city (Fig. 5). Also in Oregon, the Portland chapter of the Friends of Cast Iron Architecture hopes to rehabilitate their Skidmore Area with its many iron buildings, filling gaps between existing

Figure 4. Richard Morris Hunt's "Moorish style iron building." From *American Architect and Building News*, July 15, 1876.

Figure 5. Ladd & Bush U.S. National Bank, Salem, Oregon. Photo courtesy Skidmore, Owings & Merrill, Architects, Portland.

buildings by re-erecting iron fronts from other blocks that have been taken down and stored.

The Preservation of
New York Cast-Iron Architecture

A complete inventory of cast-iron buildings in New York City, with description and history of each, is being prepared by the Friends of Cast Iron Architecture, a national group organized in 1969 for the purpose of recording iron architecture and arousing appreciation of it which will, it is hoped, lead to its preservation. The New York Landmarks Preservation Commission has assembled records on some of the iron buildings, and has received the information on all types of buildings in the SoHo section gathered in 1971 by a group of students from the Pennsylvania State University College of Arts and Architecture. Certain dates and names of architects that appear in the present volume have come from these sources, but most of the information in the book is drawn from old municipal records, early photographs, real estate books and architectural periodicals.

In scanning the Friends' inventory of iron buildings, it is sad to see the frequency with which misguided owners have violated the design of the ground floor of these buildings in order to make them "look more up-to-date." In some cases it is apparent that the iron columns and supports have actually been replaced by new materials, but in other cases they have merely been disguised, covered by "modern" substances. In the latter instances, owners would be able to remove the covering and restore the iron to view once more.

Most fortunate of all are the many buildings whose design integrity has been respected. A great number stand with roof cornice fully in place, most or all of the small decorative elements intact, and the ground floor virtually unchanged. One example is 93 Reade St. (p. 13); another is 112 Prince St. (p. 63).

Many of the iron-front buildings cry out for decent maintenance. Even two of the iron buildings which have been designated as landmarks are sadly in need of care—the Haughwout Building (p. 142) and the former Bond St. Bank (p. 90).

On the other hand, many iron fronts are kept painted and in good shape. Among them are the landmark 75 Murray St. (p. 8), 361 Broadway (p. 130), 453 Broome St. (p. 48), 90 Maiden Lane (p. 4), 101 Spring St. (p. 57), 1 Bond St. (p. 88), 109 Prince St. (p. 61), 118 Franklin St. (p. 24), 26 East 14th St. (p. 102) and the old Stern's department store on 23rd St. (p. 118). Then there are "the Greene Street Blues," the three Second Empire-style buildings on the east side of Greene just north of Canal, whose owner has painted them, mansard roofs and all, swimming-pool blue.

According to the City's Landmarks Law, a public hearing must be held before a building can be designated as a landmark. Many of the iron buildings shown in this book, outside SoHo, could be designated instantly inasmuch as hearings on them have already been held. As for the others, now that the Landmarks Law has been strengthened to permit public hearings year round on call of the Commission, I urge its Chairman and members to recognize the unique richness of the City's heritage of iron architecture and to protect it before it meets the fate of similar buildings in Baltimore, Cincinnati, St. Louis and Chicago. In those cities the iron buildings were demolished before 19th-century architecture had come into full appreciation.

The Landmarks Preservation Commission has taken the long-awaited and welcome step of designating SoHo as an Historic District. Fortunately the decision was made by the city to protect the entire 26 blocks of SoHo on which public hearings were held in July 1970, instead of only a smaller core area. The designation,

voted on August 14, 1973, affects the district bounded by Canal St. on the south, Houston St. on the north, West Broadway on the west and Crosby St. on the east. Crosby is little more than a service thoroughfare behind the buildings on the east side of Broadway, most of which extend through the block to Crosby. This boundary therefore embraces the many important buildings on Broadway between Canal and Houston Sts.

There is wide community awareness of the historic and architectural value of SoHo. Time and the developer have somehow passed by this area of lower Manhattan, so that it still remains as a characteristic 19th-century commercial district. SoHo should be upgraded, iron-front and masonry buildings alike rehabilitated, gaps in the street scene filled in compatibly and all new construction guided by a City plan so that it is appropriate, in good taste and, above all, in the best interests of the City. The artists who have won the right to live in their spacious loft studios in SoHo have attracted art galleries, interesting eating places and even a bookstore. The SoHo Artists Association states that the artists seek to live in harmony with the small industries that have long functioned in the SoHo loft buildings. These small industries, providing jobs for many unskilled workers, are a significant ingredient in the city's economic life, so mixed uses of the buildings in SoHo will be encouraged.

Every effort should be made to get SoHo's iron-front buildings into the hands of appreciative owners. Many will continue to be loft and factory buildings, like 453 Broome St. (p. 48) and 109 Prince St. (p. 61). Others will be acquiring suitable new occupants if artists continue to "co-op" them, converting the lofts to work-in—live-in studios and perhaps the ground floors to galleries. Unexpected adaptive uses may present themselves, as was the case in 1972, when a new owner of the old McCreery Store on Broadway, the three Elghanayan brothers' firm, decided to renovate it as a luxury apartment house. The work was well advanced in the spring of 1974.

The outlook for iron buildings is better today than it was even a few years ago. Up to that time, considered beneath notice and utterly expendable, they fell before bulldozers in many center-city urban-renewal clearances.

The Landmarks Commission in New York City is custodian of some iron components removed by the

Telephone Company from the old buildings that once housed textile firms along Worth St. Besides these, there are the celebrated 1848 Laing Stores that stood on Washington and Murray Sts. and are regarded as being the first of the prefabricated iron fronts (p. 11). They were disassembled in March 1971 with Housing and Urban Development Agency funds under the auspices of the Landmarks Commission. With great care the parts were cleaned, numbered and stored for re-erection within the campus of the Manhattan Community College scheduled to be built on their site.

In New York City much of the challenge still lies ahead. Can the city handle SoHo creatively, reinforcing its character and special qualities and upgrading it as a resource to the entire community? Even more difficult, can it survey and identify its unequaled heritage of iron-front buildings throughout lower Manhattan and then, using such tools as zoning, granting of air rights, landmarks designation, tax abatement and other means perhaps yet to be devised, stabilize these remarkable structures for future generations? Hopefully New York can achieve a better record of preserving its innovative 19th-century iron structures than Chicago has with its historic early skyscrapers.

Margot Gayle

March, 1974

140–142 PEARL ST. (1869, addition 1876, Griffith Thomas). This is the southernmost cast-iron front still standing in New York City. It was actually erected in two sections at two separate times. The section numbered 140 Pearl is much the older of the two. It was a brick-tea warehouse until 1869, when the well-known architect Griffith Thomas was engaged by the owners, Oliver S. Carter and Henry E. Hawley, to make it into an office building. He not only enlarged it by extending it through the block to Water St., but gave it a new face on the Pearl St. side—a streamlined cast-iron facade. Expanding again in 1876, the owners had Thomas erect a matching five-story iron-front section on the adjoining lot at 142 Pearl St. Using identical iron castings, he added a fifth floor to 140 Pearl and unified the two sections with a single bracketed and arched cornice.

In 1873 the Rockefeller brothers, John D. and William R., established here the very first Eastern office of the great Standard Oil Company, remaining here until 1882. For decades restaurants have been housed in the lower portion of this building, where tea used to be stored. Best known of these was the famed Loufre's, whose name can still be discerned in the arched cornice. Since 1936 the restaurant has been the Chateau Tavern, owned by Melvin Fergang.

63 NASSAU ST. (c. 1860, James Bogardus?). On busy old Nassau St. stands a narrow cast-iron building that passersby never notice. For one thing, two retail stores are jammed into a "modernized" ground floor. For another, a fire escape rather masks the upper four floors of cast iron. This must have been a dainty pastiche when it was new and painted a light color to simulate stone. Fluted engaged columns rise the height of the three upper stories, supporting keystoned arches bordered by rope moldings. Between the arches are foliated spandrels, and a highly ornate cornice marks the roof line. On the subordinate cornice above the second floor rest the bases of the tall columns, and here we find an unusual decoration not noted elsewhere in the city. It takes the form of bas-relief portrait busts framed in wreaths. Benjamin Franklin is depicted on two of the columns and George Washington on the other two (see details, right).

There is every reason to believe that the old building behind the cast-iron front was the residence and shop of Augustus Thomas, who made spectacles, silver thimbles and pencil cases in the 1830s. Later he shifted his line of business, selling kitchen furnishings here until 1859. Then the building changed hands, and apparently its new owner, bootmaker Julian Gauton, had it refurbished. As so often, we have an instance of an up-to-date cast-iron front being added—in this case just before the Civil War—to an old structure in order to spruce it up for commercial purposes.

James Bogardus was such a trend-setting figure in American architecture that every effort should be exerted to identify all existing examples of his work. We know his earliest buildings have been demolished, but it is reasonable and quite tantalizing to think that there are several of his somewhat later buildings standing unrecognized even now in downtown Manhattan. For example, the ornate little cast-iron front at 63 Nassau St., to which we give a date of about 1860, may well be a Bogardus product. Its period is his period, and its style his style. Comparison of this building with certain known Bogardus buildings may lead to at least a tentative identification. Stylistically, it is a close cousin of the iron-front 1860 warehouse at 85 Leonard St. (see p. 21), where Bogardus' own trademark is molded into a metal window ledge. Both buildings have multistoried fluted columns, arches with faceted keystones, yard after yard of rope molding around windows, foliated spandrels enframed in more rope molding, and an overall sense of fussiness. Moreover, 63 Nassau can be compared with two other very famous Bogardus buildings that have disappeared: the Harper & Brothers printing plant, built in New York City in 1854, and the big Baltimore Sun Building, erected in 1851. These two buildings not only had the multistoried arches between fluted columns, elaborate cornices and a highly decorated quality; more important, their columns also rested on square bases bearing identical sets of bas-relief portraits of Benjamin Franklin and George Washington enwreathed in scroll work. The conclusion that 63 Nassau is a Bogardus building is intriguing and should stimulate further study.

90 MAIDEN LANE (1872, Charles Wright). This is a handsome piece of symmetrical design with very large plate-glass windows on its first three floors. It has little decoration other than a bracketed cornice, small capitals on engaged columns between the windows, and arched windows in the end bays. The mansarded fourth floor has a series of dormers. The iron castings were made in the famous foundry of Daniel D. Badger, whose trademark, "Architectural Iron Works, NY," is barely legible through layers of paint at the bases of the four piers of rusticated quoins.

The two older buildings behind this front were 94 Maiden Lane, where Cornelius Van Schack Roosevelt, an importer of fine glassware, had had his store since 1815, and 90-92 Maiden Lane, which he and his son, James Alfred Roosevelt, acquired in 1869. Roosevelt's building, which extends through the block to Cedar St., was purchased in 1911 by the Continental Insurance Company. During World War II it was loaned to the Coast Guard for use as a barracks. At present it is used for the storage and distribution of printed matter. Great credit is due to Continental for preserving it and maintaining its architectural integrity.

BENNETT BUILDING, 93 NASSAU ST. (1872, Arthur D. Gilman). When James Gordon Bennett, Jr., came into control of his late father's sensational penny newspaper, the *New York Herald*, this impressive status-symbol building, bearing the family name, was nearing completion. It stood back-to-back with the flamboyant Herald Building, put up by the elder Bennett in 1866. Famed Boston architect Arthur D. Gilman designed the large 93 Nassau St. office building in cast iron—six floors of identical units of very individual contemporary design. It stretched a-

long Nassau from Fulton to Ann Sts., its iron facade wrapping in a smooth curve the corner of the block at each of these streets.

Young Bennett sold the building in 1888 for a price of $1,600,000 to John Pettit, who added four floors of castings exactly matching the original iron. Very few of the iron elements are still apparent in the ground floor. However, at one place on the Fulton St. side can be seen an iron-clad pier (above left) with quoins whose decoration suggests a flow of molten lava, maybe melting ice, or perhaps a small cascade.

POTTER BUILDING, PARK ROW & BEEKMAN ST. (1883, Nathan G. Starkweather). On the night of January 31, 1882, a disastrous fire, in which several lives were lost, destroyed the old World Building that stood on this choice site overlooking City Hall Park. Orlando B. Potter, leading New York real estate investor, immediately commissioned Nathan G. Starkweather to prepare plans for a new, utterly fireproof building. Starkweather had just completed for Potter a building intended to be a hotel, still to be seen at the northeast corner of Broadway and Astor Place (see p. 159). A report of the times said that the new Queen Anne style Potter Building on Park Row, made "of brick, stone, and iron, was so constructed that it would endure practically forever." There is a great deal of cast-iron work on its first two stories, the massive brick piers being clad with iron plates of ornate design. The major entrance on Beekman Street is signalized by the cast-iron pavilion shown in the photograph above, only the upper two of its three floors having escaped concealing alteration.

The Park Row frontage has a great deal of beautiful work. In the photo opposite we see the great second-floor windows, which occur in pairs divided by slender square pilasters and topped by peaked pediments. Each of the five pairs of windows on the second floor appears between heavy structural piers which are clad with iron on the first and second floors and become brick on the upper floors, and which dominate the small-scale window details. The segmental arches seen at the base of the photograph relieve the overall geometric squareness of the building. One could say that the architecture is vigorous and masculine, and the decorative details delicate and feminine.

Much pseudo-Colonial detail appears on this overelaborate pile of dark red, which was once part of celebrated Newspaper Row, housing for many years the editorial office of the *New York Observer*. It shouldered the former New York Times Building, now Pace College, while farther north stood the great Tribune Building and Pulitzer's World Building. Sandwiched between the latter two stood the New York Sun Building, a mansard-roofed structure which had been modernized from ancient Tammany Hall. An iron founder's label is bolted onto the southeast corner of the Potter Building. It reads, "J. M. Duclos & Co., Iron Works."

75 MURRAY ST. (1857, James Bogardus?). This is one of the earliest and best-looking of the cast-iron fronts existing in the city. It is one of three cast-iron buildings officially designated as landmarks by New York City's Landmarks Preservation Commission. Richly detailed in the Italianate style, it was built for Francis and John Hopkins in 1857 to house their glassware business and was painted a light color to simulate stone. All of the columns, large and small, are fluted and must at one time have had Corinthian capitals, although the leaves have been stripped away. A strong horizontal emphasis is given by an elaborate cornice at each floor and by a crowning cornice with large decorative brackets.

The arched windows on the second and fourth floors have volute-shaped keystones, while the keystones on the third and fifth floors are shaped like the head of the mythical Medusa. Medusa keystones absolutely identical with these appear on two existing Bogardus buildings, and his 1848 Laing Stores (see p. 11) displayed similar Medusa heads, as probably did his own Duane St. factory. Furthermore, Bogardus himself says in his 1856 promotional pamphlet that F. Hopkins & Brothers, glassware, was one of the firms for which he had already erected one iron building at 61 Barclay St. May not this Venetian palazzo be a Bogardus building?

Above: HOBOKEN FERRY TERMINAL, BARCLAY & WEST STS. (c. 1890). The once busy Hoboken Ferry House at the foot of Barclay St. functioned around the clock, inasmuch as the Lackawanna ferries ran day and night. Carrying 100,000 passengers daily, these picturesque boats plied the Hudson River between the Lackawanna Railroad's terminal in New Jersey, and this and other terminals on the Manhattan side. The ferry house was made with an exposed steel frame sheathed in thin corrugated iron. Its upright steel members were anchored in bedrock beneath the water. The buckling of the iron has caused a waviness that is referred to as "oil canning." The terminal is no longer used, and trash is piled in the entrance where vehicles used to pass onto the ferries—first, horse-drawn wagons, and later, autos and trucks. Built before the turn of the century, the ferry house has attractive low, sweeping lines, although there is little decoration beyond acroteria at the ends of the roof and on the top gable, and round-headed windows bordered by squares of colored glass. Ferry service here ended in 1969, and the building, deteriorating every week, has suffered a fire as it awaits demolition in the shadow of the World Trade Center.

Opposite: LAING STORES, WASHINGTON & MURRAY STS. (1848, James Bogardus; not standing). This was New York's first cast-iron building, erected for Edgar Laing, who earlier had a coal yard here. Put up as a single building, it was subdivided into five separate stores. Its

novel aspect was the use of modular iron parts, bolted together to create the walls on the two street frontages. The rest of the construction was traditional with brick load-bearing walls and wooden floors.

The basic unit was a large window flanked by attached, fluted Corinthian columns, which supported a horizontal member or lintel. The windows were double-hung sash above a paneled spandrel area. The two outer walls consisted of this motif repeated, 24 times on the Murray St. side and 27 times on the Washington St. side. The rather elegant curve at the corner contained the motif at every floor level. Star-shaped sunburst designs in cast iron lay within the pairs of sunken panels in each spandrel, while a curved foliated cast-iron design enhanced the horizontal members and served the functional purpose of covering the joints between them. These seam coverings consisted of a scroll design terminating in a Medusa head.

Later the Laing Stores housed produce concerns. In the 1960s a sweeping urban renewal action doomed the historic building, and the area was razed by the spring of 1971. The priceless real estate on which the Laing Stores stood was turned over for the projected Manhattan Community College, in exchange for which its parent institution, the City University of New York, agreed to reerect this landmark building within the college complex. The iron sections were disassembled with the utmost precision and placed in a storage area nearby, where they await resurrection.

50 WARREN ST. & 120 CHAMBERS ST. (before 1865). Although three versions of this cast-iron front were constructed in New York City, this one, built for W. H. Jones in the early 1860s, is the only one that survives. O. B. Potter put up a similar building at 501 Broadway just north of Broome St., that recently gave way to a parking lot, while John Dolan had the third erected on Broadway at the southeast corner of Worth St. Dolan's building disappeared when a huge site was cleared for the new Federal Building in the 1960s. 50 Warren extends through the block to Chambers St., where an identical facade is to be seen. It is unusual in that the windows are separated by two-story pilasters which support strongly defined cornices above the third floor as well as at the roof line. The round-headed window arches, which rest on small attached columns, have foliated decoration in their spandrels. D. D. Badger cast the iron for the three buildings, which, looking much more ornate than here, appear as Plate XC in his catalogue.

93 READE ST. (1857). The center building above is an extremely dignified cast-iron front of five stories topped by an elaborately modeled cornice. It appears as Plate XV in the 1865 catalogue of D. D. Badger's Architectural Iron Works (see illustration, right). The Reade St. version was erected for John Jones in 1857, the year after the iron Cary Building, seen to the left of it, and also in Badger's catalogue, had been built (see next page). Today's skyscrapers have scarcely more glass surface than this Italianate facade. Identical fluted Corinthian columns stand five across at every story, diminishing in height from floor to floor. They have been stripped of the leafy Corinthian capitals which show clearly on the plate in the catalogue. The ground floor has 14-foot-tall arched windows and doorway, while on the top floor the arched windows are repeated with the addition of volute keystones. Five consoles support a large entablature and cornice with an arched pediment that emphasizes the slender height of the building.

CARY BUILDING, 105–107 CHAMBERS ST., 89–91 READE ST. (1856, Gamaliel King & John Kellum). Here is a cast-iron building of enormous importance, for it is probably the oldest iron building in the city. It has broad identical facades on both Chambers and Reade Sts., and stretches through the entire block. Every effort has been made in the design to create an iron building that looks like stone. The wall areas appear to be rusticated masonry, and the columns, cornices and arches are treated exactly like stone. The castings, so crisp and well-defined, were done in D. D. Badger's Architectural Iron Works. His foundry mark cannot be found on the building because the lower floor has been drastically altered, but a reproduction of the Cary Building appears as Plate VII in his 1865 catalogue (opposite). Plate VIII depicts the de-

tails of the Corinthian capitals and the ornamental arches. Late in 1973 the building was refurbished with new shops, bright mod awnings and a coat of white paint.

Coupled, fluted Corinthian columns which have lost their acanthus leaves support semicircular arches which have lost their keystones. The overall design consists of one arcaded row on top of another for a full five stories over which extends a cornice supported by heavy scrolled brackets. In its pedimented center appears a cartouche with the name of the owner. This was an office building with stores on the ground floor for Cary, Howard & Sanger, fancy goods merchants. It was assessed at the time at $80,000.

171 DUANE ST. (1859). This serene cast-iron building gazes down upon tiny Duane St. Park. A three-story Federal house of 1828 forms the basis of the building. There is evidence that when the area ceased to be residential, the house was raised to five stories and the iron front put on, transforming it into an up-to-date commercial building. The date of this "modernization," 1859, can be inferred from the fact that the base of one of the piers shows a foundry label of Jackson and Throckmorton, who were partners for two years only, 1858 and 1859. Furthermore, that was the time when the tax assessment on the property increased sharply due to alterations.

This iron front at the northwest corner of Staple St. is organized vertically with soaring four-story arches. Detailing is very flat and geometric. M. J. King, a wholesale egg firm which owns this dignified small building, has carried on its business in it for nearly half a century.

The brick wall (above) is part of the Staple St. side. The iron shutters apparently were hinged onto existing windows, as can be assumed from the Federal-style stone lintels. Originally, a one-room schoolhouse stood on this corner of Staple St., which is only two blocks long and appears on very early maps of the area.

Right above: 172 DUANE ST. (1871). One of the very few two-story iron fronts in the city overlooks Duane St. Park. Its modest Italianate facade, with three tall arches surmounted by three lesser arches, has enriched spandrels. Decorative capitals once topped off the paneled pilasters, but these capitals are now gone. Erected a century ago for John Copcutt, a dealer in mahogany whose business was around the corner on Washington St., the old building houses the World Cheese Company in this neighborhood of butter, egg and cheese wholesalers. This market enclave, once part of the extensive Washington Market section, remained when most of the area was cleared for urban renewal following the Market's move to Hunt's Point in the Bronx.

Right below: 12 HARRISON ST. (detail). Near the Hudson River, in the heart of what used to be the old Washington Market area, stands a 19th-century commercial block at the edge of a cleared urban renewal area, where high-rise apartments are under construction. Both sides of this block on Harrison St. between Hudson and Greenwich Sts. are lined with unpretentious red-brick buildings having the old-style loading platforms and sheds suspended over the sidewalks. It is still a functioning produce neighborhood, and from the fading names on the buildings, appears to be a "cheese block." At 12 Harrison, where we see the name "Continental Cheese," is a very plain six-story structure with a ground floor made entirely of cast iron. The major supports are of sternly good-looking design and between them closes a long, flat series of pleasingly proportioned iron doors such as those shown in our picture. The panels of the doors are outlined in a running stylized leaf pattern. The paint is peeling; the look is beat; yet they do have style. This block has an integrity and ambience that suggest a potential pedestrian shopping street adjacent to the big urban renewal project.

147 WEST BROADWAY (1869, John O'Neil). On the southeast corner of West Broadway and Thomas St., the Towers Cafeteria occupies ground-floor space that has been modernized with contemporary materials. However, a glance at the four stories above the cafeteria suggests a 19th-century commercial building of masonry. But no—official City Building Department records show that in 1869 this structure was erected as a new building, not of smooth, hewn blocks of stone with neat quoins at the corners, but of cast iron (perhaps a thin veneer over a brick front). We are accustomed to seeing iron buildings with columns, porticos, balconies and so forth, which deceive the beholder into accepting them as stone, but we are not at all accustomed to seeing this smooth effect of ashlar achieved in the protean cast iron. A careful scrutiny from the street discloses rusted iron areas showing through peeling paint. Also, the pedimented window lintels, with their incised decoration, show no chipping or disintegration as might be expected of stone, and the same is true of the almost mechanical regularity of the rusticated quoins at each side of the facade.

The moment we recognize this building as iron our thoughts fly to two small buildings in SoHo at 91 & 93 Grand St. (p. 40), which boast cast-iron ashlar facades similar to this one and which were erected in the very same year, 1869. In the case of the Grand St. buildings, the well-known architect John B. Snook seems to have ordered the twin iron fronts from the J. L. Jackson & Brother foundry catalogue. Perhaps architect John O'Neil did the same thing in the case of 147 West Broadway, but now that the ground floor has been completely remodeled, any chance of finding a foundry label is gone.

8 THOMAS ST. (1875, J. Morgan Slade). A very chaste iron front for a ground-floor store (above) that gives no hint of the High Victorian Gothic aspect of the four floors above it (right), where round-arched windows surrounded by alternate black and white voussoirs rest on polished marble columns, creating a different-sized arcade on each floor. Here, the strong Ruskinian feeling suggests that the young American architect may have had a British model. However, he could have found inspiration for his building in Withers and Vaux's Jefferson Market Courthouse, then under construction in Greenwich Village and now a public library. This part of Thomas St. was once the tree-shaded lawn of the old New York Hospital, established before the Revolution. When the hospital moved and the grounds were cut into building lots by the New York Real Estate Association, 23-year-old Morgan Slade was commissioned to design this building for David S. Brown & Co., a long-established firm of soap manufacturers. Brown & Co. stayed at this address until almost the turn of the century.

Noteworthy cast-iron elements in the ground-floor design are the very slender columns that stand on high bases and are topped by tall impost blocks, and the very tall paneled iron doors which can be folded back into the recessed wall at either side, giving entry to the upper floors. Such a favorite is this little building, in an area where all else has been torn down, that there is some talk of reassembling the facade in the courtyard of some museum. Why is it not a landmark?

Despite his youth—he was only 31 years old when he died in 1882—Slade did several commercial buildings which are still standing, among them four others of cast iron (pp. 27, 31, 61 & 154).

Opposite: 41 WORTH ST. (1864). An unusual five-story iron front, off the beaten track and thus seldom noticed by admirers of the city's iron architecture, stands on the north side of Worth St. between Church St. and West Broadway. The startling element in its design is the heavy rope molding crossing the face of the building at every floor line. "The rope pattern is peculiarly well suited to the casting process, and is particularly advantageous in making large castings," wrote architectural historian Henry-Russell Hitchcock in 1954, adding, "The ribbing which the ornament provides strengthens the various members more effectively than would merely thickening them." He was writing about the 1849 Coal Exchange in London. On 41 Worth St. a thinner rope molding lines the inside of the round-headed windows, whose arches spring from slender fluted columns that have lost the little iron leaves from their capitals. As an added surprise, a miniature urn is set atop each window's keystone. Exposed wall surfaces above the windows are grooved to look like ashlar masonry. Faceted quoins clad the strong piers that sustain the outer edges of the front. Since 41 Worth St. was erected before Buildings Department records were kept, its date of origin, 1864, has been arrived at by a study of tax records, as has been the case with many of the earlier buildings depicted in this book. The 1864 date is further substantiated by an old photograph of another building of nearly identical design that stood at 137 Broadway. It bore the date 1863 in its fancy arched roof cornice. Perhaps 41 Worth once had a similar super-elaborate cornice with big urns at either side of a central hood-like arch. The cornice on both buildings is supported by large consoles displaying lions' heads. This might be a Bogardus building.

Right & next page: 85 LEONARD ST. (1860, James Bogardus). Now that James Bogardus' Laing Stores lie in disassembled pieces awaiting uncertain reincarnation (see p. 11), 85 Leonard St. is the one and only positively identified Bogardus structure known to exist in New York City. The grandfather of cast-iron architecture in America, Bogardus was the man who envisioned the prefabrication of sections of buildings in cast iron and the assembling of these sections into facades or even whole buildings, as was the case with his own factory at Centre and Duane Sts. 85 Leonard is a warehouse with a five-story front of iron, the rest of the building being of conventional brick and wood construction. Fortunately for us, Bogardus put his label twice on the front of it, so that now its origin can never be questioned. Even though one of the labels, the rectangular plaque shown on the next page, was recently pried loose from the base of a column, a second label, which can never be gotten loose, is embossed into the iron window ledge at the left of the front door. It is 48 inches long by an inch and a quarter wide and says, "James Bogardus, Originator and Patentee of Iron Buildings, Pat., May 7, 1856."

Since Bogardus was more of an inventor than a designer, his facade for 85 Leonard seems overly elaborate, as though he enjoyed encrusting an iron front with decoration. Here we see slender two-story fluted columns, which once had leafy Corinthian capitals, standing on paneled bases and carrying arches trimmed with rope molding and keystones. Cast-iron lions' heads anchor the cornice across the third-floor level, while on the top of the building, four bearded faces stare down from a bracketed cornice.

Could it be that James Bogardus saw 85 Leonard St. as providing him with an opportunity to expound on the decorative possibilities of cast iron? The details at the top of the building almost comprise a catalogue page, displaying such samples of enrichment as twisted rope molding, modillions, imposing consoles, corbel blocks, the spandrels'

foliated scrolls, faceted keystones, an egg-and-dart trim, a top edging of stylized water leaves and, gazing out above it all, bearded faces.

Since around the time of the Civil War, Leonard St. has been a street of sales offices for wholesale fabric concerns. Then as now they were housed in the buildings with all or partial iron fronts which we see today. 85 Leonard is occupied by a refolding company that unwinds yardage of cotton jersey from great reels and folds it onto small bolts.

Below: BOGARDUS TRADEMARK. Iron founders often put their trademarks in plain sight—very plain sight—right on the front of the build-

ings for which they produced the iron architectural elements. Here is the trademark of the famed James Bogardus, and it is the only one of his trademarks of this bolt-on type to be seen in New York City, where it is believed he erected scores of iron buildings. Until recently it graced the base of a Corinthian column at 85 Leonard St. (see preceding page). Then it was removed and with the permission of the owner presented, handsomely mounted, to the Landmarks Preservation Commission, which for obscure reasons voted not to designate this significant building as an official city landmark. Such designation should be conferred as soon as possible.

JAMES BOGARDUS, ORIGINATOR, AND CONSTRUCTOR OF IRON DINGS. NEW YORK

83 LEONARD ST. (detail). As though by arrangement for a class demonstration of how some cast-iron buildings were constructed, two side panels of a column pedestal have been removed. Probably knocked loose by a truck, the natural enemy of the cast-iron loft building, one panel has disappeared, and the other leans against the standpipe. The main thing to note is the vigorous inner cast-iron column support. It is doing the actual work of holding up the building, while the fluted cast-iron outer column jacket is just for good looks.

116–118 FRANKLIN ST. (1869, Griffith Thomas). After the Civil War, Samuel D. Babcock, a Wall St. banker, had the popular architect Griffith Thomas design two commercial buildings for sites on opposite sides of Franklin St. between Church and West Broadway. This five-story building on the north side of the street clearly carries Thomas' imprint. That is to say, it is a utilitarian edifice whose great flat-arch windows admit a maximum of light, and whose smooth three-quarter-round columns of decreasing height support a marked cornice at each level, the final roof cornice being held on large brackets. It has a pronounced checkerboard facade bordered on each side by piers defined by rusticated quoins. The building, painted a medium gray, is well maintained by its owner, who operates the famous Teddy's Restaurant around the corner and who owns several other pieces of property close by. The ground floor is rented by Stewart Dickson Marine and Industrial Packings, a firm that has moved from the one-time shipping area along South St., where glass skyscrapers are replacing the old Greek Revival warehouses.

As early as 1808, Franklin St. appeared on city maps with the name Sugar Loaf St., because of the sugar warehouse which stood in the middle of the block between it and Leonard St. In 1816 Sugar Loaf St. was renamed Franklin St. in honor of Benjamin Franklin.

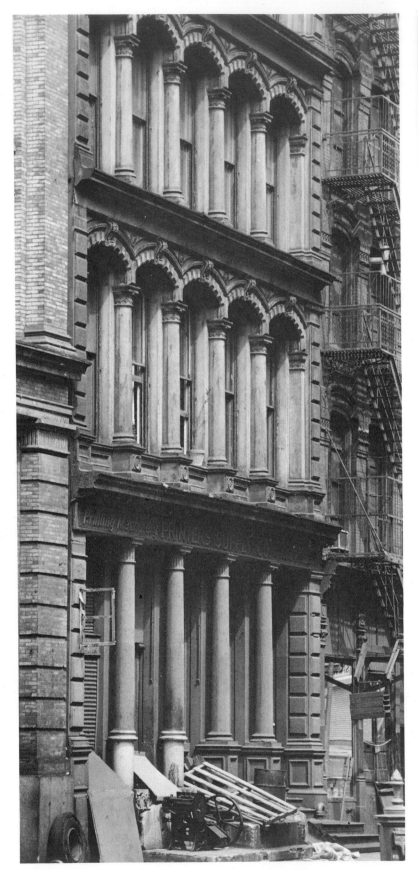

8–10 WHITE ST. (1869, Henry Fernbach). Two experienced professionals put together this cast-iron building. They were Henry Fernbach, the well-known architect (whose work is also represented on pp. 61, 71, 81 & 119), and Marc Eidlitz, the well-known builder. Although the first floor has been abused, and some of the iron pedestal plates are missing, we can see pretty clearly what Mr. Fernbach intended. The tall, free-standing first-floor columns stand on high bases, making possible a daylight basement. A stoop of six steps leads to the main floor. The window units that make up the upper four floors are nearly identical except that the columns lessen in height toward the top of the building. Photographed at an angle, as here, they show up as one bold arcade above another.

A prominent cornice completes the building, and is needed to match the vigor and uniqueness of the strongly modeled facade—the fully round columns at the ground level and the smooth three-quarter-round columns on boxy bases at the other levels, as well as the heavy segmental arches over the windows, composed of what might be called rusticated voussoirs with acanthus-leaf keystones (see detail above).

The street level is occupied by the Printers Supply Company, the second floor by a machinery mover contractor, while upper floors appear to be divided into several loft apartments.

86–88 FRANKLIN ST. (1881, J. Morgan Slade). This loft building got its last coat of paint, a flaking reddish brown, some years ago and has a rather oppressive green fire escape. Still, it stands out on Franklin St. near Church St. as a utilitarian building with a lot of class. Perhaps the building's appeal lies in its good proportions, perhaps in the architect's imaginative application of classical details. Four windows are grouped in a center section with slim little columns between them, free-standing except for a decorated iron membrane that holds each to the fa-cade. On either side of the four-window bay is a single window flanked by the heavy structural piers bearing minimal stylized decoration. The deep-set windows give the flat facade a sculptured effect through con-trast of shadows and light. Every window on the face of this structure is of the same design, except that the windows grow smaller toward the top. This was a device of great interest to the designers of these 19th-century buildings. Large scrolled brackets support the final cornice, which is topped off by a big triangular pediment.

55 WHITE ST. (1861, Kellum & Son). D. D. Badger, the famous iron founder, displayed this building as Plate CII in his 1865 catalogue, *Illustrations of Iron Architecture*. He had manufactured the iron front early in the Civil War according to specifications of Kellum & Son, architects for the Condict brothers. Samuel I. and John Elliot Condict moved their large saddlery into the building at once. Later it was used by various textile concerns, for many years by a drapery company, and for the last 25 years by a firm of cotton jobbers and converters.

Five stories tall with a basement and a sub-basement, 55 White St. has a bold facade with a double tier of giant arcades. The solid–looking columns, two stories high, sustain round arches over the windows. As depicted in Badger's Plate CII, the arches originally had keystones, and the columns terminated in Corinthian capitals. Also lost are the faceted quoins on the corner pier, such as those still to be seen at the right edge of the building. One learns, by observing these lost details, what a multitude of separately cast parts were combined to create a total iron facade such as this. More than one owner has become impatient when these small decorative castings have come loose, and, rather than have them reattached, has ordered, "Get them all off; they'll never be missed." But the truth is, with the growing appreciation of the city's iron architecture, they are being missed.

Kellum's bold iron front, 73 feet and six great windows wide, has many cousins in the immediate neighborhood. Although by different architects, all were built within a few years of one another in this popular tall-arcaded style. Go and look at 388 Broadway, 392 Broadway, 504 Broadway, 80 Leonard St., and even 85 and 87 Leonard St. All are kissing kin, and a few are almost identical. Some are of stone, some of iron. Who was copying whom?

Opposite: 60 WHITE ST. (1869, D. C. Williams). A perfect example of a post–Civil War commercial building, devoted then as now to the wholesale textile trade. For some years around the turn of the century, it was occupied by Albert G. Hyde & Sons, dealers in cotton goods, especially linings, who moved from here to a more prestigious address on Broadway, eventually locating in the big building at 361 Broadway (p. 130). The tradition is carried on by the Rosner Silk Company, which deals in fabrics, a firm operated by the second generation of a family that owns the building and has operated here for nearly half a century. An arresting view of this building is secured by looking north along little Franklin Alley squarely at number 60 on the uptown side of White St. The ground floor has tall fluted Corinthian columns on either side of a central doorway which is reached by a four-step stoop. To the left of the door is a show window, to the right a loading entrance with roll-down shutter. Tall pilasters, with almost unadorned, recessed panels, form the building's margin on either side. The large three–abreast windows on each floor have flat arches and double–hung sash. In the big cornice, held by four heavy brackets, an arched central pediment, topped by an urn, displays the date 1869. This building is a twin to the building adjacent on its easterly side, number 62 White St., and a cousin to number 64, which is wider. All three, which share party walls, are close relatives to 385–389 Broadway just around the corner (p. 134).

Right: 83–85 WHITE ST. (1881, J. Morgan Slade). Architect Slade designed this building in a quiet utilitarian style not unlike that of 109 Prince St. (p. 61). In both buildings he provided a maximum of window area to light the interior. Perhaps no other cast–iron building in New York City has "all its buttons" to a greater degree than this one. The fire escape is a later addition, as is the air conditioner, but otherwise the original owner of this commercial structure, attorney William P. Dixon, could look at it today and find it the way he had had it built 90 years ago. It even retains a flagpole above the ground floor and rolling metal shutters to close the ground–floor shops at night. These bear the imprint, "Cornell Iron Works, Long Island City." The 50–foot–wide building is painted a solemn forest green and is very well kept.

254–260 CANAL ST. (1857, James Bogardus?). In this impressive iron building, the deep reveals of the windows, their large and shapely keystones, the fluted three-quarter-round columns, the marked string courses of the balustrade and the cornices are characteristics which Henry-Russell Hitchcock described as "the very vigorous relief which the taste of the mid-1850s generally demanded." This very large pre-Civil War building, with iron fronts on each of its two sides, stands at the southwest corner of Canal and Lafayette Sts. It is rather severe in design when compared with such other early iron-front buildings as 75 Murray St., 85 Leonard St. and the Haughwout Building (pp. 9, 21, 142), yet it is truly Italianate and certainly in the palazzo mode, which had been introduced to New York in A. T. Stewart's 1846 marble store, still to be seen at Broadway and Chambers St. On the facades of the Canal St. building, a quiet equilibrium is established between the horizontal cornice line at each floor together with the cornice on brackets at its roof line, and the vertical lines achieved by the upward-thrusting columns beside each window.

In 1832 George Bruce, one of the early developers of Canal St., bought the corner from Peter Jay Munro. Burnt out early in 1856, he then put up this iron-front building to accommodate stores and warehousing.

The Italianate semicircular arches of all 28 windows on the fourth floor have Medusa-head keystones (left). This seems to have been a favorite architectural motif of James Bogardus (see p. 9). These keystones strengthen the feeling that this is one of the many Bogardus buildings which once lined the streets of New York. The conviction grows when one considers the Venetian design of the building, for we know that Bogardus was inspired in his invention of iron fronts by the buildings of Venice.

268 CANAL ST. (1886, Lansing C. Holden). On the edge of expanding Chinatown, at the southeast corner of Canal St. and little Cortlandt Alley, stands a six-story cast-iron loft building which houses several clothing manufacturing firms operated by Chinese businessmen. In 1871 Jeremiah W. Dimick, a merchant in worsteds and wools, moved to a small structure on this site from around the corner on Walker St. Later he replaced his small building with this large iron-front store and loft building, moving his own carpet store to 501 Broadway, a more fashionable location.

The iron front is 50 feet wide with a 17-foot return on the alley, the remainder of alley frontage being a plain brick wall. The square-headed windows are very wide indeed, each separated from the other by a free-standing slender iron colonnette. The third and fifth-floor colonnettes support an entablature with a slightly protruding cornice. The second and fourth-floor windows are surmounted by spandrels decorated with ornaments like fanciful snowflakes. At the fifth floor a series of decorated panels extends across the facade under the roof cornice. The sixth story, above this cornice, was quite clearly added later. The ground floor of 268 Canal has been altered to a great degree, but the piers on the right and left sides of the structure still carry their quoining and bear iron founder's labels. These read, "Atlantic Iron Works, 706 E. 12th St., N.Y." In any other city, this building and its neighbor at 254 Canal would be acknowledged landmarks.

351–353 CANAL ST. (1871, W. H. Gaylor). On busy Canal St., at the northeast corner of Wooster St., the Brooklyn architect W. H. Gaylor created a large five-story palazzo warehouse with two sides almost entirely of glass contained in large, segmentally arched windows. There is a harmonious balance between horizontal and vertical lines, and the decoration is quite reticent. It is a splendid example of cast-iron construction making use of identical prefabricated parts. The extremely tall first floor, so popular in the 1870s, has not been altered, and the building, except for the addition of fire escapes, must look much as it did when it was constructed. It was orginally built for stores. Then, 50 years ago, it housed a large auction firm, while now it is occupied by the Tunnel Machinery Exchange. At the Canal-Wooster corner of the building, there are identical foundry labels reading "Bailey & Debevoise, N.Y."

27 HOWARD ST. (1888, Samuel Warner) & 29 HOWARD ST. (1868, Renwick & Sands). Two cast–iron buildings stand shoulder to shoulder on Howard St., gazing northward up little Crosby St. They were built 20 years apart, both designed by famous architects. That on the left in the picture opposite is a neat utilitarian structure which Samuel Warner designed as a store for Samuel Inslee. Its austere post–and–lintel construction allows the utmost window space, except for the top floor, where a rather naïvely placed arcade consists of five small round–headed windows. The Victorian–looking structure to its right was built shortly after the Civil War by Renwick & Sands for Edward Matthews. Howard St. was named for Harry Howard, a brave volunteer fireman from his teens until the end of his life, by which time he was the famous Chief Engineer of the Volunteers. Note the charming cast–iron bishop's–crook lamppost, which has just been replaced by a modern high–intensity street light.

At the right is a detail of 29 Howard. Renwick & Sands eschewed the classical vocabulary and built a pretty Victorian store and warehouse with two floors of cast iron and three upper floors of marble. Only by looking beyond the obtrusive fire escape can one discern the small–scale decorative elements—flowerlets, festoons and the very light stylized design at the top of the first floor. In the central entranceway, a rolling iron shutter shows us how these iron fronts could be closed up securely. It is interesting to note that architects of this period lavished originality and care on small commercial buildings as well as on large commissions. For example, the year after doing this building, Renwick & Sands won accolades for their prestigious Second Empire style Booth Theater, 23rd St. at Sixth Avenue. Renwick, of course, did St. Patrick's Cathedral and Grace Church.

Collection Margot Gayle

50–52 HOWARD ST. (1861). During the Civil War this double–width iron and masonry building, with its very tall and well–proportioned fluted Corinthian iron columns, was occupied by the New York State Soldiers' Depot, a rest home with a hospital ward on the top floor for Union soldiers on leave from the front. Built the year the war started for Adam W. Spies, a dealer in guns, it cost about $25,000, and was brand new when pressed into service for the Soldiers' Depot. The Depot opened in July of 1863 and was depicted in *Valentine's Manual* for the following year as a significant public building (illustration above left). Although it has been abused, nothing seems to have been removed from it since Major & Knapp made the 1864 lithograph for Mr. Valentine showing the cast–iron columns and their entablature painted a milky white, the four floors of white marble above unsullied, and a large Union flag streaming from a second–floor pole. Thus, in the light of what we know about it, we can readily people it with uniformed soldiers and lady volunteers in crinolines, and evoke a sense of its earlier importance. After the war the building became the William A. Stokes & Co. woodenware store. Somewhat the worse for wear, it is presently used by the Rivoli Company, notions wholesalers. The building is larger than it looks at first glance, for there is an L–shaped wing opening onto Mercer St. at number 16 that also has four stories of marble above iron Corinthian columns on its first floor. The dignified ironwork for the Depot was produced in the J. L. Jackson Brothers foundry on Goerck St. The iron rolling shutter over a door between the columns at the extreme right of the facade on Howard St. is still there, though stuck tight with paint. Just across the street was an entrance to Mr. Arnold's Department Store (later Arnold Constable), which faced on Canal St. and gave the neighborhood great class.

83–87 GRAND ST. (1872 & 1883, William H. Hume). A long impressive shot down Greene St. shows only cast-iron fronts. The same can be said of the opposite side of the street. In the right foreground stands an impressive iron warehouse with a handsome range of four columned floors above a tall ground-floor colonnade of 11 free-standing columns with Corinthian capitals. Architect William H. Hume did it in 1883 as a silk showroom and warehouse—an addition to that section of the building, just out of sight to the right of the picture, which had been erected 10 years earlier. Perhaps it was part of an original grand plan, for the architect had the iron elements for this big addition cast in exactly the same design as for the first building, resulting in a unified whole. The older part of the building carries the date 1872 in its galvanized iron cornice, and displays the foundry label of Lindsay, Graff & Megquier. 25 years ago the great sheets of plate glass that had allowed light to flood into the groundfloor showrooms of the silk warehouse were taken out and replaced by glass brick. The brownish, weatherbeaten building is now used as the factory of the Baker Brush Company, the Company's entrance being in the contiguous 1872 part of the building at 79 Grand St.

Opposite: 91 & 93 GRAND ST. (1869, John B. Snook). J. L. Jackson & Brother operated a large foundry that turned out architectural ironwork for many years. They patented a simple design for iron fronts intended to look as though these were of ashlar construction, which is to say constructed of large flat-faced stone blocks. We see two examples made to this patent at 91 & 93 Grand St. between Mercer and Greene Sts. The houses were built with crude brick fronts onto which the iron was applied as large, thin rectangular plates. These have iron pins on their backs, the pins reaching through the brick wall to be anchored by flat bolts on the inside of the house. So precisely are these plates fitted that the seams cannot be detected from the street. They are grooved, of course, to look like uniformly sized pieces of cut stone laid up with mortar. Window ledges are of iron, as are the segmental arched lintels above the windows. This veneer-like handling of iron plates on a facade brings to mind one of the earliest examples of iron architecture in America, the little bank in Pottsville, Pennsylvania, for which in 1832 John Haviland ingeniously dreamed up an iron-plated front because no good-looking stone was at hand. Our small, matching, 20-foot-wide, four-story buildings on Grand St. were erected together in a mere four and a half months during the summer and fall of 1869. It seems to have been a very efficient job, and inexpensive, too, as the cost for each

was around $6,000. Although built for two different owners to accommodate small stores, they had the same architect—none other than the prominent John B. Snook, whose name was associated with the St. Nicholas Hotel nearby and the first Grand Central Station. A machinist firm owns and occupies number 91 Grand St., which it has painted a light green with dark green trim. Several young families own cooperatively and live and work in number 93 Grand, which they plan to paint when they have finished work on the inside. Small oval founder's labels, no more than four inches long, are attached to the outer piers of the buildings. These read: "J. L. Jackson & Bro. Iron Works, 28th St.—2d Ave.—29th St" (illustration below).

Right: 89 GRAND ST. (1885). Slender attached columns with very pretty stylized capitals done in a Furness-like free interpretation of the Romanesque. Supporting decorative impost blocks, these columns comprise the ironwork on the first floor of a commercial building at the southeast corner of Greene and Grand Sts. They must have been cast in the same molds as the iron columns across Greene St. at number 31 and those a block away at 72 Grand St., as they are all identical. The upper four stories of the building are brick, and it has a graceful overhanging metal cornice held on molded brackets. The Opokovis Restaurant occupies the ground floor.

Above: 419–421 BROOME ST. (1873, Griffith Thomas). At least half a dozen large cast-iron buildings still stand scattered along Broome St. as monuments to the skill and popularity of Griffith Thomas. He was the son of Thomas Thomas, a London-trained English architect. "By 1860 the firm of Thomas and Son had become one of the busiest in the country," according to architectural historian Winston Weisman, who states that between 1868 and 1873 the firm was responsible for 33 large office buildings, insurance companies and banks. The five-story commercial structure pictured here apparently was one of these. It stands between Crosby and Lafayette Sts. on the periphery of what we think of

as the cast-iron district. We see some of Thomas' characteristic touches: the rusticated quoins of the side piers, the segmental arches, wide expanses of glass, and the use of cast-iron balustrades to embellish a facade. He was not one for overexuberant cornices, and the pressed tin cornice here, held on brackets and surmounted by a central arched pediment, is quite decorous. Why isn't this a landmark?

Right: 425–427 BROOME ST. (1874, Edward Kendall). William Bloodgood, a Pearl St. merchant, had a pleasant residence at 425 Broome St. around 1850, and the Rev. James McElroy was his next-door neighbor. Like so many New Yorkers, Mr. Bloodgood watched commercialism moving up Manhattan Island and took advantage of the fortunate location of his real estate by having a large commercial building erected where his house once stood. To do this, he bought out the Rev. McElroy, so that in 1874 he could commission architect Edward Kendall to build a five-story warehouse for him. It has a modern-looking iron and glass front on the south side of Broome St. at Crosby, where it wraps around the corner. It looks quite modern because a great deal of the surface is glass, divided into large square-headed windows by slender colonnettes. These colonnettes, with

reeding on the lower part and stylized, small-sized capitals, stand on high pedestals and support tall, thin impost blocks. These are marked by a rosette and a bit of curving incised trim. Alessi Brothers, Inc., use this building for storage of the office furniture which they sell in a retail store in the financial district. Probably for this reason, they give little attention to the building's appearance. The windows are dirty, and the iron cries out for paint.

Opposite: 433 BROOME ST. (c. 1865). Here is a friendly and likeable four-story cast-iron building with windows so wide that only three can be fitted across each floor. Three-quarter columns, unadorned except for Corinthian capitals, are echoed by similar pilasters on either side of the building. The glory of it all is a baroque ornamental cornice held on four large brackets. There is a fancy centerpiece with a finial, above which rises an arched pediment topped with a cast-iron urn. The building is occupied by the West Side Electric Company, electrical contractors specializing in motor installation. To be sure, its proportions are a little daft, yet this is one of countless admirable iron-front buildings which would have been demolished had the horrendous Lower Manhattan Expressway been constructed.

Right: 435 BROOME ST. (1873, W. A. Potter). This building stands like a great Eastlake-style bookcase on the south side of Broome St. just east of Broadway. It rises five narrow stories to a cornice suggesting Victorian furniture, with pointed arched windows that have cusped tracery, and with the date 1873 barely legible in the peaked pediment. For all this, it attracts few glances, because of interest in the celebrated Haughwout Building across the street (see p. 142). No two cast-iron buildings could be more different than these, for the Haughwout is an Italian palazzo with serried arched openings and delicate classic décor. Buildings like 435, which cry out for a coat of paint and a good scrubbing of the windows, are far from derelict, housing active businesses, in this case the Best Socket Screw Company.

Above left & right: 448 BROOME ST. (1875, Frederick Clarke Withers). A dainty stylized floral design veils the slender metal elements of the glass and iron facade of this five-story cast-iron warehouse created by an English architect who left his mark on New York City with the Jefferson Market Courthouse, now the Greenwich Village branch of the New York Public Library. For John Jacob Astor, Withers did the elaborately carved reredos in Trinity Church. His "feel" for overall carved surfaces is exemplified in his one and only iron-front building. Before a fire escape was placed across its front, the building had a very pretty cornice of iron filigree along the roofline with finials at either end and ironwork interwoven into a peak at the center.

Opposite: 464–466 BROOME ST. (1861). In the first half of the 19th century, SoHo developed from a sparsely settled area to a busy residential community with schools, stores and churches. On the northeast corner of Broome and Greene Sts. stood the charming little Broome St. Reformed Protestant Dutch Church. In 1861 the building in our photograph went up on the site. Its owner, Aaron Arnold of Arnold Constable's department store, bequeathed it to his son and his daughter Henrietta, the wife of James Constable. The stunning tall, fluted iron columns on its first floor were cast in the Nichol & Billerwell foundry on West Houston St.

453–455 BROOME ST. (1873, Griffith Thomas). The popular Griffith Thomas created this building originally for Welcome Hitchcock's silk and veilings store. Thomas gave the building five floors of Corinthian columns of diminishing height which flank broad rectangular windows with rounded corners, all handled in his characteristic manner. Characteristic, too, was the course of balustrades that tops his dignified, tall ground floor. The sixth story, a true classic attic, was originally crowned by finial-tipped cast-iron urns, another Thomas favorite. Piers with rusticated quoin blocks add weight and stability at the corners. After years of neglect, the building was renovated by its appreciative present owner, Architob Millner, a bottler of olives, who continues his restoration work.

Opposite: Here is Cast-Iron City!—the blocks on the south side of Broome St. between Mercer and Wooster Sts., with a full range of five-story iron-front loft buildings. These buildings were erected between 1870 and 1885. The architects created harmony with a similar treatment of the iron fronts and a nearly uniform cornice line.

469–475 BROOME ST. (1871, Griffith Thomas). The tier–on–tier of broad windows under flattened arches, the regular placement of columns between the windows, stories decreasing in height and marked at each level by a very positive cornice—all typify Thomas' style. On this building, erected for William H. Gunther, one of New York's foremost dealers in furs, the cornice at the roof protrudes considerably, held on very strong decorative brackets. Originally it was crowned by a balustrade with urns. Thomas often used decorative balustrades, and here we see a cast–iron balustrade girdling the second–floor level above a first floor of very tall three–quarter–round attached Corinthian columns. At one time what look like mere shelves protruding at the fourth floor were balustraded balconies, with three urns apiece. On the Broome St. side, we find a pedimented doorway that may once have been the building's main entrance, for its columns support a large broken pediment which must have held another urn—what else? It brings to mind the similar doorway, broken pediment and all, which can be seen in old photographs of the store that Thomas did five years later for Arnold Constable on Broadway at 19th St. At the western end of the building is a hard–to–decipher foundry label of the Aetna Iron Works.

The most eye–catching thing about this building is the elegant curved treatment of its corner. This effect could only have been gained in cast iron, for the curved treatment of flattened arches could scarcely have been achieved in stone. Between piers with rusticated quoin blocks, there is on each floor a curved window, those on the second and third stories still containing their expensive curved panes of glass. The building carries its name in what looks like a cast–iron tiara above the second floor, and in its days of glory, two cast–iron ladies, greater than life size and draped in classical garb, stood on what were actually pedestals at either side of the Gunther nameplate. Only the pedestals remain, and one cannot but wonder who is keeping the ladies now. All this style and quality for a warehouse! Recently 10 people who appreciate this stunning cast–iron building have acquired it as a co–op. There are to be art galleries on the ground floor and live–in artists' studios on upper floors.

This was probably a silk wholesaling area, as next door stood the Cheney Brothers' silk warehouse, while the year 1900 finds William Schroeder & Co., silk importers, occupying the ground floor of Mr. Gunther's building and the Liberty Silk Company also leasing space in it as a sales room for the dress silks which it manufactured in its factory on West 57th St.

Opposite: 476–478 BROOME ST. (1872, Griffith Thomas). A very Griffith Thomas building! On this building and on his 453 and 469 Broome (pp. 48 & 50) are to be observed the strong, smooth columns, all with Corinthian capitals comprised of precisely cast acanthus leaves, standing between very large windows with characteristic flattened arches. Each floor is emphasized by a strong cornice line, and the stories are of diminishing height, beginning with an extremely tall and open ground floor. The architect's visual legerdemain makes this iron facade appear to have a central pavilion rising to its pediment on the roof. This is achieved by the use of three-quarter-round columns in the center section, whereas the side portions of the facade have flat pilasters. Since the building is L-shaped, one can walk around the corner from Broome St. to Wooster St. and see an identical though narrower iron front. The building now houses the Standard Paper Box Machine Co, in whose window a sign says, "Metal Work Done for Artists."

Right: 477–481 BROOME ST. (1885, Elisha Sniffin). The Cheney family had already produced artists and authors as well as successful businessmen when they erected this iron-front building to house the sales and distribution headquarters for their large silk company. A photograph of the building that was printed in 1902 could be retaken today, except for the awnings at many windows and the cast-iron urns and balustrade along its roof line. This structure, which looks almost like a pair of twins, has a very tall first floor with five upper stories of decreasing height. The windows are large with flattened arches and double-hung sash. In each of the twins, small balustrades at every floor level and a pediment in the cornice give the merest suggestion of a central pavilion. The double building, apparently fully rented and prospering, has a fresh coat of paint, slate-blue upper floors with ground floor of bolder blue. This building by Sniffin relates well to the Griffith Thomas building adjacent on its eastern side, the floor levels coinciding neatly. It is to the credit of these architects that they sought not so much to make an unforgettable statement as to create street architecture in harmony with its surroundings.

485 BROOME ST. (1872, Elisha Sniffen). When architect-builder Elisha Sniffen erected this building on the southwest corner of Wooster and Broome Sts., it was a five-story affair with a cornice of galvanized iron. Some drastic things have happened to it in a hundred years. The cornice and the top two floors were taken off, probably in 1903, leaving what we see today, a three-story brick building minus cornice. Its ground floor is supported by quite handsome rectilinear iron pillars with chamfered corners which have interesting Romanesque capitals of furled leaves, but are otherwise quite austere (detail left). They stand on square bases, each bearing the label of the Atlantic Iron Works (detail below). This foundry, which, like the many others in Manhattan, has long been out of business, was at 706 East 12th St. near the river, where coal and iron could be conveniently brought in by boat.

The building is empty. Recently it was advertised for sale at an asking price of $90,000. It is interesting to note that in 1885, 13 years after 485 Broome St. was completed, Sniffen did number 477 (preceding page), in a very different style, for the Cheney Silk Company.

500 BROOME ST. (1874, Charles Mettam). A neglected, rather large building with a narrow iron facade on Broome St. that wraps around the corner wall onto West Broadway, where the rest of the long wall is made of brick. There is a typical front platform for deliveries, and it is not hard to imagine horse-drawn drays backed against it for loading. The first floor, painted black just after our picture was taken, has an old rolling iron shutter at the door and the address numeral 500 cast right into the corner piers. It bears three foundry labels reading "Aetna Iron Works, 104 Goerck St., N.Y."

A cornice at every floor level makes its way around the strong iron-clad corner pier and, protruding markedly, creates a very harsh profile. The building stands five stories high and has flat-topped windows, with arched corners, separated by three-quarter-round engaged columns. Charles Mettam, the architect of this building, was very enthusiastic about iron as a building material. Not only did he design iron buildings for several clients, but he took out at least one patent improving the system of joining cast-iron members. For over 30 years, Thomas Barrett & Son, paper manufacturers, had their office and warehouse in this building.

101 SPRING ST. (1870, Nicholas Whyte). An elegant building with two sides of iron and glass. The iron elements are of extreme slenderness, and the ornamentation is handled with a very light touch. Delicate engaged colonnettes clustered at the corner of this building mask a strong supporting pier (see detail on next page). The architect, appreciating the nature of his material—its tremendous strength in compression—employed iron for iron's sake, and not in imitation of stone. This allows the exterior walls to consist almost entirely of glass. Surely it foretells today's glass–walled skyscrapers.

This is an owner–occupied structure in SoHo. It belongs to sculptor Donald Judd and his wife, Julie, who is a ballet dancer. The one–time commercial building provides great high-ceilinged areas for large–scale sculpture on the lower levels, and spacious living quarters on the upper floors for the Judds and their small children. (Further detail p. 178.)

121 SPRING ST. (1878, John B. Snook). This is another John B. Snook building. The more we study the background of the individual structures in SoHo, the more we encounter this architect's name. Here at Spring and Greene Sts. is a typical 25-by-100-foot corner-lot building combining the benefits of cast iron for the store front with the conventional five-story structure of brick. The most conservative businessman in the 1870s could go along with this combination. There is not much to be said about the cast iron on the ground floor of this building. It is sensible; the details are eclectic; the upkeep is miserable. The iron work, now a weather-beaten green, was provided by the J. B. & J. M. Cornell Foundry. The Standard Casing Company, which has its business here, produces the Stancase Stainless Steel line of food-handling equipment.

Left & above: 151 SPRING ST. (1889, John B. Snook & Son). On the north side of Spring St. near Wooster St. there are two six-story brick buildings which have cast iron on the ground floor. Our concern is with number 151 Spring, where the cast-iron pilasters are modeled with sunken panels bearing symmetrical stylized floral decoration. The treatment of the capital is very archaic: acanthus leaves lined up side by side, then surmounted by a length of egg-and-dart molding. More interesting is the numeral "151" for the street address custom-molded across the waist of the pilaster. The Manhattan Scale Company, which builds and repairs big weighing devices for factories, occupies the ground floor here, while upper floors house a designer of far-out plastic furniture and a painter.

Opposite: 109 PRINCE ST. (1882, J. Morgan Slade). This large utilitarian cast-iron warehouse occupying the northwest corner of Prince and Greene Sts. was built 90 years ago at a cost of $80,000. Since 1943 it has been occupied by the Industrial Hardware Co., a large firm which manufactures parts for TV sets and is typical of the many stable industries in the SoHo area. This company also occupies 121 Greene St., seen just to the north in the photograph, which was also built in 1882 but after designs by Henry Fernbach. Both buildings are kept in fine repair and have just been painted a yellow-beige with forest green on the ground floor and cornice. The strong horizontal lines of 109 Spring St. are created by a cornice on each floor resting on smooth square pillars. The chamfered corner gives a certain distinction and emphasizes its corner entrance. An iron founder's label, which says "Architectural Iron Works, Cheney & Hewlett," can be discerned on the base of a column on its Greene St. side.

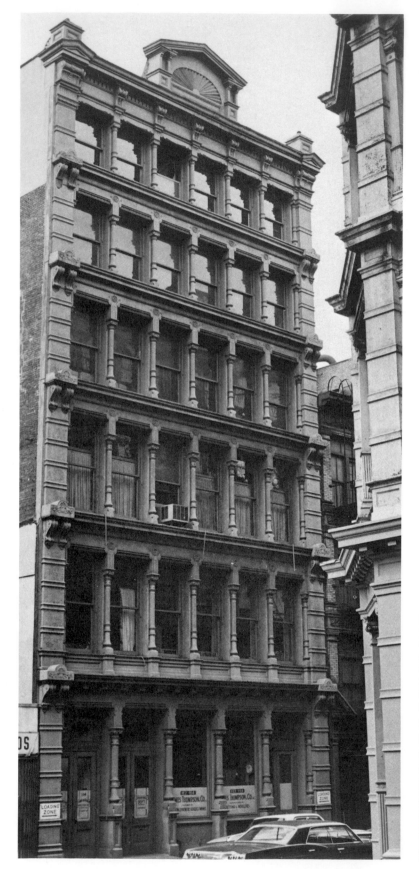

Opposite: 112 PRINCE ST. (1889, Richard Berger). Prince St. was going commercial in a big way in the 1880s. The building seen at the right edge of the picture at the far left, 109 Prince St., was put up in 1882, while that facing the camera, 112 Prince, was erected during the latter half of 1889. Both are utilitarian warehouse types, which have always served industry and continue to do so, even though the neighborhood is experiencing an influx of artists and art galleries. The building on the right houses a firm manufacturing TV parts. That on the left is occupied by fabric concerns, one of which is James Thompson & Co., finishers of cotton and synthetic goods. The latter's 40-foot all-iron facade has great square-headed windows with double-hung sash separated by slender attached colonnettes. These have stylized capitals, stand on pedestals and support tall impost blocks topped by decorative rosettes. The strong horizontal line at every floor is created by a protruding cornice anchored at both ends by a decorative block supported by paired consoles. At the roof the cornice has a tiny pediment at either end and a central raised pediment which shelters a sunburst design. Iron fronts such as that at 112 Prince St. usually support only their own weight and are attached to otherwise conventional structures with load-bearing brick walls. The photograph shows this rather clearly. Here the brick side wall has virtually no windows, as it was anticipated that an equally tall building would one day be erected alongside this one.

The ground floor (photo immediately opposite), a study in Victorian eclecticism, maintains its 1889 look. To be sure, the pedestal of a column alongside its loading entrance has suffered an accident and had its side patched with sheet metal. But today it is so difficult to have matching portions cast to replace broken parts that one can only applaud an owner who has conscientiously had the broken metal even crudely patched and painted over.

Right: 472 WEST BROADWAY (detail). A bit of floral fantasy on the first-floor iron pilasters of a brick warehouse just south of Houston St. These iron columns have been painted a pinky beige.

Left: 470 WEST BROADWAY (detail). A sunflower grows on West Broadway. Raise your eyes to the top of the first–floor pilasters at number 470, and you will see a pleasing design with a centered sunflower on a bed of stylized leaves. Plate–glass windows between the pilasters and beneath the dentilled cornice have now been blocked in and stuccoed over. The whole first floor, iron and all, has been painted a pinky beige for its tenant, a folding paper box factory.

Opposite: 381–383 WEST BROADWAY (1876, John B. Snook). This is an old loft building six stories tall—taller than most in the neighborhood. It is one of several big warehouse–type structures with a 55–foot frontage on both West Broadway and Wooster St., running a full 200 feet through the block. The ground–floor cast iron is similar to that of other buildings nearby, providing a very tall, open first story. The decoration is minimal, the square pillars which clad the inner structural supports having sunken panels with diamond–shaped insets. It is a series of these piers across the front of the building which holds up the yellow brick front wall—five high–ceilinged stories of it. The building is on the eastern or older side of West Broadway, 25 feet having been lopped off the other or western side when the street was widened in 1870. Evidently the building dates from an earlier period, when the street was called South Fifth Avenue and the numbers began at Washington Square. The tip–off is the numeral cast into the pillars that frame the door of 381 West Broadway. It says "161" and signifies that this was 161 South Fifth Avenue. On the doorway to the north, the numeral is "159." SoHo is full of warehouses or factory buildings not unlike this one, which have several floors of lofts—that is to say, attic–like space not partitioned off into rooms. These lend themselves to manufacturing processes, to the installation of machinery and to storage, and in recent years have become studio space for artists, many of whose expansive sculptures and vast canvases require lots of space.

Opposite: 392–394 WEST BROADWAY (1872, John H. Whitenack). A cast-iron industrial building that has served its function well and still does. Erected a century ago as a loft building, it is straightforward and open in design, with a flat surface and a maximum of window space. The five stories of almost rectangular windows are framed by rusticated quoins up the sides and a fine projecting cornice held by brackets. In the centered pediment arch are faintly discernible the numerals "1872." This building and most of its neighbors on the west side of the street were erected after its widening in 1870, sometimes on portions of remaining foundations.

Right: STREETSCAPE, WEST BROADWAY SOUTH OF SPRING (378–380 West Broadway, 1873, Edward H. Kendall; 386–388 West Broadway, 1871, Robert Mook; 392–394 West Broadway, 1872, John H. Whitenack). These three cast-iron buildings were erected on the raw new western margin of West Broadway soon after the widening of 1870. As this was a wholesale and, later, an industrial area, architectural stylishness was not necessary to attract retail customers, so the ground floors of these buildings have remained "unmodernized." West Broadway had first been named Laurens St. for Henry Laurens, president of the Continental Congress. After its widening it was called South Fifth Avenue, with numbering running south from Washington Square. Sometime in the 1890s the name was changed to West Broadway, with numbering running from south to north. Then, in the late 1950s City building czar Robert Moses tried to rename it Fifth Avenue South as an asset to the urban renewal project south of Washington Square. He bowed before local opposition, just as, recently, the City's cultural administrator August Heckscher bowed after he had proposed renaming some of its blocks for artist Jackson Pollock. At least one change has stuck, however, the name La Guardia Place for the section between the Square and Houston St. Commercial art galleries have followed the influx of artists into SoHo, and there are galleries in all of the big cast-iron buildings shown here. The full rehabilitation of 380 West Broadway, with its J. L. Jackson Brothers foundry label, has changed the exterior very little beyond a good paint job, but interior alteration has created superb live-in studios for artists. 386 West Broadway, which has a foundry mark of Novelty Iron Works, Brooklyn, was built for Amos R. Eno, the fabulous entrepreneur of the first Fifth Avenue Hotel on Madison Square. Number 392, housing diversified manufacturing, was built for Jeremiah W. Dimick. Each of these three iron-front buildings originally cost between 30 and 40 thousand dollars.

35–37 WOOSTER ST. (1866, Samuel Curtiss, Jr.). Tall fluted Corinthian columns, free-standing and elegant, comprise the first floor of one of the finest-looking old commercial buildings in SoHo. The four upper stories are of brownstone very carefully detailed in the classical mode, uncluttered by fire escapes. The roof cornice of cast iron has a broken central pediment that holds a cartouche, atop which probably stood a figure or at least an urn. At the base of the supporting elements, with their rusticated quoin blocks at each end of the facade, one finds the foundry mark of Nichol & Billerwell, 234 West Houston St. When architect Samuel Curtiss designed the building for stores in 1866, there was every promise that its neighborhood would be one of consequence for years to come, yet by 1868 nearby Arnold Constable's big store was pulling up stakes and starting the trek of retail business uptown. An envelope manufacturing company now makes good use of this building. If its surroundings seem drab, there is a bright note in the youthful exuberance of the actors and musicians who have turned the garage next door into an off-Broadway theater dubbed the Performing Garage.

99 WOOSTER ST. (1886, Napoleon Le Brun). This three-story red brick and limestone building has cast iron on the first floor only. The iron is painted bright red. The upper story has tasteful insets of molded red terra-cotta, while the seemly cornice appears to be held by giant pilasters at either side of the building. Carefully handled stone courses make their way across the second story, unifying the three-window facade. The small, skillfully designed building looks as though it might once have been a rich man's stable, yet this seems unlikely in a warehouse district. Inquiry discloses that it was originally a firehouse built in 1886 as the home of Engine Company 13, which had succeeded the famous Oceanus Volunteer Engine Company when the fire service was transformed into a professional fire department in 1865. The first sliding pole used in New York City was installed here by Captain Daniel Lawlor. It was taken out when Engine Company 13 moved in 1947 to historic old Firemen's Hall, its present home, at 155 Mercer St. The building is now the headquarters of the Gay Activists Alliance.

Left: 129–131 GREENE ST. (1880, detail). A brick warehouse sandwiched between two of SoHo's art galleries has a row of these slender iron columns on the first floor. They are quite daintily decorated with floral swags and stylized leaves, and stand on high pedestals with guilloche panels. This one has been cracked near the bottom by trucks backing against the loading platform, while the others are even worse off.

Above: 98 & 100 GREENE ST. (1880, Charles Mettam; detail). Quite Victorian in design, the street numbers of these two buildings on Greene St. have been cast-to-order on separate plaques bolted to adjacent paneled pilasters on five-story iron-front warehouses. Architect Charles Mettam, a public-minded leader in his profession, designed these buildings in the same year that he was diligently reforming the city's building law.

113 GREENE ST. (1883, Henry Fernbach). This is the cast-iron ground floor, painted black, of a building in the heart of SoHo that has real class in an unostentatious way. It was done by one of the city's leading architects, Henry Fernbach, who 13 years earlier had done the synagogue at Lexington Avenue and 55th St., now a designated landmark. The four iron supports of this Greene St. building, the two on either side of the door being extremely slender, are very carefully detailed. Just below the architrave is a charming art nouveau molding with a repeated motif of entwined ivy leaves. The upper four floors are brick, the first three having windows grouped toward the center and enframed with iron, while the top floor has four arches in brick with corbeling up to the metal cornice. The trim SoHo store and warehouse was built for Lippman Toplitz, dealer in caps and imported men's headware.

Above: 80–88 GRAND ST. (1881, Robert Mook). Stretching north along Greene St. in the heart of SoHo is a cast-iron vista that continues into the distance. Block after block of buildings, the majority with iron fronts, all five or six stories tall, create a nearly uniform skyline. Except for the fire escapes and the terribly dirty windows, the area looked much this way in the last quarter of the 19th century, when importers and jobbers of dry goods supplied the entire country from blocks such as these. 80–88 Grand St. (at the northwest corner of Greene St.), facing the viewer, is a large cast-iron warehouse, at once serviceable and prepossessing. For many years it was occupied by C. A. Auffmordt & Company, importers and commission merchants established in 1840, maintaining buyers in Paris and London.

Next 2 pages: 72 GREENE ST. (1872, J. F. Duckworth). The "King of Greene St." stands in the heart of SoHo, a century-old cast-iron warehouse of absolutely commanding presence. It looks down on a narrow street and is undoubtedly the hardest of the outstanding cast-iron structures to photograph. It is actually two cast-iron buildings, designed to look like one structure and unified by an imposing central portico which rises from a pedimented porch at the ground floor to a pedimented cornice at the roof. At every story free-standing columns support the protruding cornices of the portico, while on either side flat pilasters between the windows have a more subdued effect.

The central porch draws every eye and gives this building a great elegance. Four tall columns support an architrave surmounted by a broken pediment in the center of which stands a very grand urn. This type of entrance treatment must have been popular at the time. The cast-iron building at 1 Bond Street (p. 88), built two years earlier by architect Stephen D. Hatch for D. D. Appleton Publishing Company, has a similar entrance, while nearby at the corner of Broome and Greene, Griffith Thomas provided for the 1871 Gunther Building a comparable doorway at the Broome St. entrance (see p. 51). He himself may have set the vogue in 1868 with his pedimented entrance to the cast-iron first floor of Arnold Constable's store at 19th St. and Broadway. The doorway has since been removed, although the marble building exists. In the last hundred years little has been changed in the imposing facade of 72 Greene St., except for the addition of two fire escapes. It does suffer, however, from sloppy maintenance and a clutter of broken signs. This is one of several especially important cast-iron buildings in SoHo regarding which individual public hearings have been held by the Landmarks Preservation Commission, although no designation has been forthcoming. In addition, the Commission held hearings in 1970 on the entire 26-block SoHo area and eventually designated it as an Historic District in August 1973. This had long been a goal of the SoHo artists and of many civic groups and preservation societies, including the Friends of Cast-Iron Architecture.

Above: 49 GREENE ST. (1866; detail). At 49 Greene St. is an old brick building with a first floor of quite pleasing cast-iron columns and pilasters. On one of the tall three-quarter-round engaged fluted columns is a very pretty embellishment: the street number framed in a bit of scrollwork. This decoration was cast separately, then bolted on. The column is crowned by a leafy Corinthian capital, while at its base the label of D. D. Badger's famous "Architectural Iron Works" is molded into the plinth.

Right: 46 GREENE ST. (1860; detail). Twin protruding iron pilasters stand at the first-floor level, where the walls of adjoining loft buildings meet. Scrollwork and ornate medallions are bolted onto the long panels, which are flanked by receding panels that once concealed tracks for roll-down metal shutters. The Corinthian capitals of the two pilasters provide a demonstration of how these were composed of separately cast acanthus leaves bolted precisely into place to create the full capital head. The capital on the left has lost several of its acanthus leaves, as so often happens when the bolts rust away. The photograph illustrates the high level of craftsmanship practiced in the best of the foundries creating architectural iron. The window areas, once glazed and secured by the shutters, are now blocked up and stuccoed. This early SoHo building, erected on the eve of the Civil War, has unusual cast-iron window enframements on its upper four stories of red brick. These enframements, together with the pilasters and fluted columns of cast iron on the ground floor, are painted a tired green. Removal—rather than repair—of the cornice has mutilated the unity of design. A scrutiny of this old building discloses the date 1860 in cast-iron numerals near the cornice line, and, molded into a column plinth, the foundry label "Jackson & Throckmorton."

32 GREENE ST. (1873, J. F. Duckworth) & 34 GREENE ST. (1873, Charles Wright). A pair of cast-iron warehouses, built in a brief five months by two leading architects, near Canal St. and above all near Broadway. This section provided wholesale back-up service to the great retail establishments on the greatest street of them all. In 1873 J. F. Duckworth designed 32 Greene St., seen at the right with its bonnet cornice, as well as the mansard-topped building adjacent to it on the far right at 28–30 Greene St. (see next page). Both 32 and 34 Greene cost about the same, just a little over $30,000. They are very good companions, having their floor levels at the same height and an identical cornice line. Although quite different in detail, neither outshines the other. These two buildings have been painted the same bright blue as their neighbor to the south. The Rava family owns them all.

28–30 GREENE ST. (1872, J. F. Duckworth). This commanding Second Empire facade is surmounted by an equally assertive mansard roof comprising the sixth story, and the whole structure is painted a violent blue. There is a great dignity to this facade, which has tall, broad windows under segmental arches with keystones. Between the windows stand half-round attached columns with bell-shaped capitals from which the decorative acanthus leaves have been stripped. A central bay of two windows, emphasized by free-standing columns, runs the entire height of the building. It is capped by a broken pediment above which rises the central mansard pavilion. The dormers in this mansard are incredibly fancied-up with balustrades, keystones and pediments with modillions and finials. Artists occupy the lofts.

Above: GREENE ST. LOOKING NORTHEAST FROM CANAL ST. All of the buildings on both sides of this block are iron-front constructions by such "name architects" as J. F. Duckworth, Charles Wright, Samuel A. Warner, J. Webb and Henry Fernbach. Here we see the eastern side, where three of the large buildings—numbers 30, 32 and 34—have been painted a very lively and very bright blue. This contrasts with the facade of the structure at the right, number 20–24, which for years has worn a coat of washed-out dark brown paint. The buildings can be seen to great advantage, because interior fireproofing has made fire escapes across the front unnecessary. The ground floors are used for industry while lofts on upper floors are rented as live-in, work-in space to many artists.

Opposite: 20–24 GREENE ST. (Samuel A. Warner, 1880; detail). Part of the great cast-iron scene as one goes up Greene St. north of Canal. Samuel A. Warner designed two large mirror-image twin warehouses for this site, which is three building lots wide. To this day they serve as factories with their exteriors so little changed that they look just as they did when they were built. Even the street in front, with its Belgian blocks and cast-iron manhole, shares in the 19th-century look. This photograph shows the identical piers running up the entire height where the two buildings abut one another.

15–17 GREENE ST. (1895, Samuel A. Warner). One of the many good-looking and carefully detailed cast-iron warehouses done by the successful architect Samuel A. Warner. Across the street are 16–18 Greene St. and 20–26 Greene St. (p. 79), also by Warner, both built in 1880. Some architectural historians solemnly write that cast iron went out in the 1880s, so please note that the building in our picture was erected in 1895. It is now an artists' co-op, the lofts partitioned into studios and living quarters. Observe the house plants on the window sill.

19–21 GREENE ST. (1871, Henry Fernbach) &
23–25 GREENE ST. (1872, J. F. Duckworth).
Here is typical cast-iron street architecture: flat
fronts relieved by tiers of columns and windows deeply set, producing a surface play of
light and shadow. The last building on the left
is shown on the opposite page. The center
building, number 19–21 Greene St., was built a
hundred years ago as a warehouse, designed
by Henry Fernbach, who did several other
buildings on this very street. To the right of it
stands 23–25 Greene, built a year later and designed by J. F. Duckworth, who at the same
time did two buildings across the street. Both
19 and 23 Greene have very tall first floors
with upper floors of decreasing height and pronounced half-round attached columns supporting flattened arches above windows so squared
off that they permit the entry of a maximum of
light. The Corinthian capitals, deep reveals and
rusticated quoins of the side piers create an undulating surface that is finished off with a mu-
tually harmonious roof line. The building near-
er us has a finial-topped pediment in its roof
cornice. Affixed to the base of one of its first-
floor columns is a plaque reading "Aetna Iron
Works, 104 Goerck Street." Should you wonder
where Goerck St. is, it has disappeared, forming part of the site for a big Lower East Side
housing project. For a quarter of a century, C.
B. Hewitt Brothers—jobbers in paper, glues and
adhesives—owned and occupied No. 23, which
still displays their sign. When they liquidated
in 1966, the building, having been sold to a
dealer across the street, became his warehouse for bales of cotton waste. Now it is about
to be converted to artist studio housing. These
two cast-iron neighbors, which went up within
a year of each other, cost around $60,000 each.

11 MERCER ST. (1870, F. E. Graef). This post-Civil War iron building was erected as the India Rubber Company's commercial warehouse in 1870. It was built for Adolph Poppenhusen, a member of the civic-minded German family that had come from Hamburg and in 1853 established the Enterprise Rubber Manufacturing Company in College Point, Queens. Among the city's designated landmarks is the Poppenhusen Institute in College Point, built in 1868 to house "a kindergarten for working class mothers and an English language school for new immigrants." As for their Mercer St. warehouse, in recent years a brush manufacturer stored bristles in it, but now the Empire Sporting Goods Company is making sports uniforms here.

The well-kept and quite handsome cast-iron front has recently been painted a medium gray. It can be appreciated much more fully because no fire escape mars its facade as is the case with buildings on either side of it (see view opposite). Number 11 has a very tall first floor and four other stories of decreasing height marked by a cornice at each level supported by smooth three-quarter-round columns. A balustrade beneath each first-floor window adds a decorative course. The picturesque roof cornice held on brackets has a central arch in which can be discerned, with patience and in a diffused light, the words "India Rubber Company" almost obliterated by grey paint. This squares with our knowledge that the building was put up for the Poppenhusens, rubber manufacturers. The iron was cast by Cornell.

47 MERCER ST. (1872, Joseph M. Dunn). Some of the old cast-iron buildings are just plain good-looking. They were when they were built, and they still are. That is the case with number 47 Mercer St., which carries the date 1872 in its pedimented cornice. To our eyes the genuine simplicity of the design is very appealing, the bold horizontal cornices at each level balancing nicely with the vertical lines of smooth round columns. How welcome the daylight must have been, pouring into these large windows with their eastern exposure, at a time when flickering gas jets were the best artificial light to be had. A second glance reveals that the paneled quoin blocks seen clearly on the right edge of the building are missing from its left edge, and that decorative capitals, probably classic acanthus leaves, have been stripped from the top of each column. The building is owned and occupied by the Decter Wool Stock Company, dealers in mill ends and wool, rayon and cotton cuttings from the clothing industry. Recently they painted their large iron-front building a pleasant medium-gray color. 47 Mercer St. looks east across a black-top parking lot on which once stood Lord and Taylor's first Broadway store (which supplemented its famed Grand St. store).

121 MERCER ST. (1879, David & John Jardine). The Neo-Grec mode, which characterizes many of our cast-iron buildings, prevailed in this city in the 1860s. It was a French taste alluding to Greek architecture through the adaptation of familiar Greek symbols to the exigencies of large urban structures. We see this mode in the very grand first floor at 121 Mercer St., which is owned by one of the many artists' co-ops found in SoHo. It has recently been painted a pale gray green, which sets off the noble height of its columns. A banding of up-ended, side-by-side anthemia surmounts the heavily reeded lower third of the columns, while the upper shafts are smooth. A careful entasis or swelling of the columns, introduced by the Greeks to offset the illusion of concavity and weakness, can be observed. Leafy Corinthian capitals support a full entablature with modillions beneath its cornice. The original occupant undoubtedly had his name in large gold capital letters along the frieze. The major supporting pier on either side of the facade has paneled quoins which at the cornice line terminate again in a large, stylized anthemion with guttae. This symbol is repeated at each floor level. The brother architects fashioned this facade with great care, and certainly the upper four stories deserve better than the rusting, peeling, dirty paint and a fire escape. (Detail p. 174.)

Above: 148–152 MERCER ST. (1860). Great big, beautiful cast-iron folding doors cover the entire first and second floors of this Mercer St. elevation, which is the rear brick wall of 577–581 Broadway (the Broadway facade is of marble). The doors have been operative until recent years, but now the hinges may be rusted permanently shut. The sections of these doors are cast in a classic paneled design giving them great dignity. They once folded back accordion-wise behind the narrow pilasters of iron. The foundry of J. R. Jackson & Co. at 201 Centre St. cast these iron doors and placed its label on them at three places. The building is on a piece of land that was part of John Jacob Astor's holdings. At one time his own home was here at Broadway near Prince St., and his one-story brick office was at 85 Prince around the corner from these old doors.

Opposite: 40 CROSBY ST. (1874, Richard Morris Hunt). A Cinderella of a building that one unexpectedly comes across on dusty, narrow Crosby St. between Grand and Broome Sts. It is the rear of Richard Morris Hunt's masterpiece iron-front building at 478–482 Broadway (p. 140). Most iron-front structures have plain-Jane brick backs, but Hunt gave this rear wall all the architectural grace of the main facade, though on a lesser scale.

1–5 BOND ST. (1871, Stephen D. Hatch). A very wide, very flat, very imposing cast-iron front built as a large office building for the firm of D. D. Appleton and Co., which dominated the publishing scene of the time. Every floor must have been drenched in light coming through the big plate-glass windows. The French Second Empire influence is evident, especially in the emphatic mansard roof with its three pavilions. The light horizontal stress of a cornice at each floor, together with bold vertical columns, make for a uniquely American grid facade. The shape of the window arches derives from ancient stone corbelling. Stephen Hatch designed another large commercial building in the French mode, the still standing Gilsey Hotel (see p. 166).

The main entrance (photo at far right) is emphasized by a projecting portico which repeats the unusual window line and is crowned by a broken pediment with a cartouche between scrolls. Surely, the Appleton name was once inscribed upon it, for the firm occupied the building for nearly a quarter of a century. Its symbol is the beribboned torch of

learning on either side of the fanlight over the front door. The first-floor columns are noteworthy for the spiral design of the lower third. A rather similar entrance treatment of a columned portico with broken pediment can be seen on the warehouse at 72–76 Greene St. (p. 73), another version at 475 Broome St. (see p. 51), and still a third enhanced Arnold Constable's old Broadway store before it was altered.

The photographic detail of the corner column treatment shows a cool and crisp design. When the Bond St. area became an exclusive residen- tial neighborhood in the 1830s, many well-known New Yorkers moved up there from lower Broadway. The home of Albert Gallatin, Jefferson's Secretary of the Treasury, stood on this site. To the right of the corner column is glimpsed old Shinbone Alley, a tiny thoroughfare laid out in 1825, which runs from Great Jones St. in a wayward fashion across Bond and Lafayette Sts., ending at Bleecker. Perhaps this double bend earned it its name, or did it lead to the mansions' stables?

OLD BOND ST. BANK, 330 THE BOWERY(1874, Henry Engelbert). The old Bond St. Bank, which later became the German Exchange Bank and after 1963 was the Bouwerie Lane Theatre, was built on the conventional 25-by-100-foot New York City building lot at the northwest corner of The Bowery and Bond St. Architect Engelbert was faced with the problem of creating an impressive bank building with only a 25-foot facade on the more important of the two thoroughfares, The Bowery. He solved this by designing an elaborate entrance on The Bowery and giving the side of his edifice on Bond St. a facade of considerable elegance, painting it a light color, as it is today. Recognizing that the viewer coming north up The Bowery got a fine view of the Bond St. facade, he devised a lavish French Second Empire creation with Corinthian columns, single and coupled, divided into bays that stressed its verticality, offset by cornices at every floor. When the bank became a theater, the windows on the Bond St. side were blocked in to darken the interior, as was a secondary entrance marked by coupled columns and by a second-floor pediment echoing the Bowery entrance.

Crowning the bracketed top cornice is a broad roof pediment. A rear service entrance can be seen with a stoop and wrought-iron railing.

The high stoop on the Bowery side, leading to an impressive main floor above a tall basement, has somehow escaped "modernization." For such a narrow front, it has a very imposing entrance with keystoned arch and tall smooth columns, the lower third of which is encrusted with a repeated anthemion design. These columns support a bold entablature with triglyphs. Too bad this Bowery facade has not received better care.

In January 1967, the Landmarks Preservation Commission designated this building as an official city landmark. Their report states that the wealth of ornamental detail, with its plastic, almost sculptural, effect, makes this building an unusually fine example of the elaborate style of the French Second Empire. Having served first as a bank, then as a loft building, and finally as a theater, 330 The Bowery demonstrates how a century-old building can meet varied needs without the destruction of its architectural integrity.

PUCK BUILDING, 295–309 LAFAYETTE ST.
(1885, Albert Wagner; 2 details). As intriguing
as an abstract painting is the alley view of the
back of this vast building with eight acres of
floor space. Built in 1885 in an eclectic Romanesque style on a truncated, pie-shaped lot,
its three facades have tall, slim rounded arches,
and its main entrance is marked by massive
polished granite columns. Outstanding brick-
work characterizes the entire building, including this handsome rear wall letting on block-
long Jersey St. The shutters are cast iron and
are custom-made for the windows—round-
headed shutters to fit the round-headed windows, squared-off shutters for the others. As a
security device, these old iron shutters, rather
inexpensive in their day, can scarcely be beat-
en. The building is admirably maintained and
is fully rented, as it has been for the past 40
years, principally by printing firms, the lower
floors being tenanted by the Superior Printing
Inks Company.

Above the door presides a large gilded metal
figure of Puck, both cherubic and foppish in
top hat and cutaway coat, contemplating himself in the mirror he holds at arm's length. He
was the emblem of the humorous weekly called
Puck that was published here for many years
in both English and German editions. Later, he
reappeared in the pages of the Journal American newspaper.

392–400 LAFAYETTE ST. (detail). Still striking in spite of encrusted paint, this artful shell pattern adorns the base of a column on a dingy cast-iron building at the northwest corner of Lafayette and Great Jones Sts. In 1806, when Sam Jones opened this byway "from Bowery Lane to the Broad Way," the Common Council gave it the name of Great Jones St. to distinguish it from the Jones St. which Dr. Gardiner Jones had recently opened on the west side of Greenwich Village.

DURST BUILDING, 409–411 LAFAYETTE ST. (1891, Alfred Zucker). The giant iron-clad piers and the two-story free-standing iron columns of this building are simply overpowering. They rise from the sidewalk like primeval trees. This brick and iron warehouse wears its abundant ornamentation like jewelry. Beaded rings ascend the columns and piers like pearl armbands, while intricate patterns enrich the horizontal panels between the second and first floors. Triple round-headed windows fill each second-floor bay.

A thriving plumbing accessory business is carried on in this extraordinary building, and, apparently, someone has a feeling for its magnificent cast iron, as evidenced by attempts to patch cracks in the column bases, where these have been hit by trucks. The building deserves to be viewed in its entirety from across Lafayette St. Above the noble first two floors of iron, there are four floors detailed with great care in a dark pink brick with terra-cotta trim. Perhaps the existing fine buildings in the area inspired architect Zucker to create this unique design for Simon Goldenberg's men's haberdashery store with tailoring workshops on the upper floors. This was the last grand commercial building to go up on this block, once replete with Astor family mansions and the Astor Library, begun in 1853, now the Public Theater. Zucker is so free-wheeling a designer that one should compare the Durst Building with his work at 484 and also 492 Broome St.

440 LAFAYETTE ST. (1870, Edward Kendall). This six-story cast-iron building was erected on virgin land that had been the garden, with a riding ring, behind the home of Mrs. Walter Langdon, whose father, John Jacob Astor, was a prime mover in developing this neighborhood. Originally the building had a mansard roof with iron cresting, and stretched through the block, having a similar facade of half this width on Broadway. The Broadway portion was demolished long ago. 440 Lafayette covers three building lots, and was built for stores and warehouses in 1870 for Charles Wood. In 1891 the crested mansard roof was removed when a sixth story was added.

The slender cast-iron colonnettes, one of which appears in the detail photo, stand between the great sheets of plate glass in the square-headed ground-floor windows. The volutes on the capitals are paired ram's horns and echo the ram's-head design that appears on the decorative shields flanking the three entrances (detail photo). The stunning shields, 18 inches in height, with a monogram, twin eagles above and a ram's head below, are to be seen on each of the six columns on the main floor. A hundred years of paint applied to the first floor, now forest green, have obscured the high relief of the shields and blurred the monogram, which is that of Alfred Benjamin & Co., a large firm established here in 1879 "manufacturing high-grade men's clothing."

Above: 444–450 LAFAYETTE ST. & 10 ASTOR PLACE (1875, Griffith Thomas). Orlando B. Potter, who acquired much property in this vicinity, commissioned Thomas to design this very strong seven-story building to house printing firms. It cast a quarter of a million dollars and was for years occupied by J. J. Little & Company, printers. In our photograph we see second-floor iron arches that rest on three-quarter-round iron columns (which once had Corinthian capitals) and that are decorated with rivet heads. Those on the third floor spring from square brick pilasters and have stylized medallions in the spandrels. An iron-balustraded balcony, which has lost its three urns, marks the center windows. The iron is painted a bluish gray that complements the warm red of the brick. Nowhere else in the city can now be found this alternation of brick and iron surfaces with their different textures.

Opposite: COOPER UNION, COOPER SQUARE (1853–1859, Frederick A. Peterson). Peter Cooper, the self-made man who had built the Tom Thumb Locomotive and shared in laying the Atlantic Cable, built Cooper Union and endowed it as a free school of technology and the arts. At his iron works in Trenton, N.J., he rolled the first wrought-iron beams in America, some of which were used in the construction of this building, which at this time is the oldest existing structure with a complete metal-frame inner core. The building's exterior is of brownstone in Italianate design with a long arcade of cast-iron arches on both the Third Avenue and the Fourth Avenue sides. The arches framing large glass windows and doorways for street-level stores, the rental of which once provided a source of revenue for the free school, were cast by D. D. Badger.

WILLIE'S GROCERY

141 7up WILLIE'S GROCERY & DELICATESSEN 7up 141

Pabst Blue Ribbon BEER

Opposite: 4–6 ASTOR PLACE (1890, Francis Hatch Kimball). This six-story commercial building stands on the site of Mrs. Walter Langdon's stables, which had been built for her by her father, John Jacob Astor. The ground floor is of cast iron very functionally handled, so as to give a broad expanse of street-level display windows. These windows are now occluded by curtains, inasmuch as the ground floor has become an annex to the Public Theater, which uses it largely for rehearsals. The architect fitted it to an L-shaped plot having a 68-foot frontage on Astor Place for its main entrance, and a 27-foot frontage on Lafayette St. with another entrance, which is opposite the Public Theater. It was originally constructed for Orlando B. Potter.

Above: 141 EAST 17 ST. (altered 1880s). Strictly this little two-story building should not be included, but it is an excellent example of an "illusion." At first glance it appears to have a cast-iron front. The first floor does have cast-iron supports in the form of fluted pilasters with stylized capitals, but the upper floor, with its pretty colonnettes and its perforated and scroll-trimmed cornice, has a front of stamped sheet metal. The grocery store and the second-floor window-walled apartment occupy an annex built in the 1880s onto an older rear building, according to architect Bernard Rothzeid, who recently renovated the structures for graphics designer Al Blaustein. The rear building, now transformed for its owner into handsome living-studio space, may have originated, according to Rothzeid, as a farm structure at the end of the 18th century.

Above: 22–26 EAST 14 ST. (1880, David and John Jardine). This big store stretches across three building lots to the east of Fifth Avenue. Its rather Frenchy ornament must have appealed to retailers who sought an air of opulence for their establishments. But the prefabricated iron is used in a logical and economical way. All the columns are absolutely identical and must have come from a single mold. Their shafts are smooth except for the lower third, which has a strapwork design and bands of upright anthemia. The capitals are a fanciful combination of garlands hung from volutes with a sunflower instead of the usual rosette. Sunflowers appear again in panels here and there on the three major uprights that support the building, and in panels on the impost blocks atop the columns on the third and fourth floors. James McCreery built this store on land which he leased from the Van Buren family. He seems never to have used it himself, but leased it to Baumann's carpet store. The ground floor presently contains McCrory's variety store. A new coat of beige paint enhances the facade.

Opposite: 106 WEST 14 ST. (1875, William Field & Son). John A. Hadden commissioned this "five-story building for first-class stores." It had an iron front and a galvanized iron cornice, and cost $35,000. It was erected in four and a half months. Today its dusty, rusty iron, its top-to-bottom fire escape and its crass first-floor remodeling for a bargain store make this a building you would not think twice about. Nonetheless, the restrained, decorative treatment of the windows is very unusual, and the cornice treatment is interesting, too. George C. Flint moved his furniture store from Hudson St. into Hadden's new iron-front building in 1876. He stayed here for 20 years before finding it necessary to push on uptown to 23rd St. After that he combined with Robert Horner.

Opposite: 34–42 WEST 14 ST. (1878, W. Wheeler Smith; 1899, Louis Korn). The Ludwig brothers had this 50-foot iron-front dry-goods store designed for them. It ran through the 200-foot depth of the block, emerging with its rear entrance at 39–41 West 13th St. The brothers enlarged their store in 1899, duplicating the earlier iron castings exactly. The result was a large uniform iron and glass facade stretching across five building lots. There is very little decoration on the building: paneled pilasters and narrow supports between the windows have stylized ornaments of classical reference. The Ludwig name was originally carried in the rectangular section of the cornice which marks the earlier part of the building, shown in our photograph. The newer section of the rear wall has cast-iron supports of a later design than those of the older portion. These carry the foundry label "John J. Radley & Co., 18th St. and E. River." The upper floors are now devoted to the manufacture of belts and handbags, while the ground floor is divided into two large stores: an H. L. Green variety store and the United Bargain Store. The later addition is the eastern half.

Above & next 2 pages: OLD B. ALTMAN STORE, SIXTH AVENUE AT 19 ST. (1876, David and John Jardine; 1887, William H. Hume). Morris Altman had this six-story cast-iron store built at the southwest corner of 19th St. but died shortly thereafter. His brother Benjamin, assuming the care of the bereaved family, moved his own business into the building and opened it under his own name in April 1877. The Jardines' designs for the store and for the unique iron castings that comprised it were sympathetically followed a decade later by Hume when he extended the store south along Sixth Avenue. Perhaps from the beginning the Jardines had had in mind a master plan providing for such expansion. Above it all, and tying it all together, was a rooftop balustrade with two ornamental arched cornice sections to signalize each of the principal ground-floor entrances. The symmetry of the design is hard to recognize now that the addition of an extra top floor to the southern third of the building has necessitated removal of one cornice arch and part of the balustrade. B. Altman & Co. moved in 1906 to its present block-square palazzo at Fifth Avenue and 34th St. (Further detail p. 179.)

The photo opposite shows a portion of the fourth floor and cornice of the earliest part of the old B. Altman's. The 1876 Neo-Grec decor is light and dainty. The whole front shares the incised single-line ornament, very much stylized in execution, which is seen surrounding this bay of three windows. Above it is a fancy entablature with brackets and, above that, a segmental arched parapet with urns and central escutcheon. A subsequent occupant, Greenhut & Co., substituted its name, now barely visible, over that of B. Altman in the cornice.

The photo above shows the original store's dramatic central rotunda. As a light court, devised in the gaslight era, it rose through six stories of surrounding galleries to a dome of glass and iron. Note the great arched iron beams enriched by pendants, filigree work and paneling. The Heckla Iron Works of Brooklyn fabricated the iron for this dome.

Above & next 3 pages: HUGH O'NEILL'S STORE, 655–671 SIXTH AVE-
NUE (1875, Mortimer C. Merritt). This impressive block-long pedimented Sixth Avenue frontage is anchored at each end by a round, many-
windowed tower. The towers were once capped by almost Byzantine
domes. Except for the missing domes, the whole thing is there today.
At its apogee the enormous O'Neill store annexed the big Adams store
on the block to its north, asserting that the two structures "comprise
one million square feet of store space, employ 5,000 persons, and
serve 100,000 customers each day." Although this leviathan contained
three floors of furniture, its real specialty was ladies' cloaks, suits,
furs and millinery. Closing its doors forever in 1915, it suffered eclipse
along with its neighbors. High in the pediment over the center of the
facade (above), big block letters bear witness to the origin of the building. Although now a reticent gray color, the building was painted a
gleaming white in the 19th century.

Harper's Weekly

Curved ends on the cast-iron facade of the big O'Neill store gave it great style, especially when each end was still topped by its dome tower as shown in the 19th century woodcut above. Opposite is a detail of one of the lower floors of a corner tower. Some of the original curved glass still remains in the windows. The store in now a loft building with light manufacturing and printing firms. These curved rooms in the towers make superb little workshops. A time-clock repair firm occupies this one.

The Sixth Avenue elevated ran in front of the store and, of course, transported many of its customers, making this location near the 23rd St. stop very desirable. But the fact remains than an unobstructed view such as that depicted in the woodcut was possible for only two or three years. The elevated service began in 1878.

EHRICH BROTHERS, 695–709 SIXTH AVENUE (1889, Alfred Zucker & Co.). Just south of 23rd St. on the west side of Sixth Avenue is a dignified cast-iron building that once housed a razzle-dazzle bargain emporium. It was run by the four Ehrich brothers, who had previously been in business on a smaller scale on Eighth Avenue. Because they wanted to be where the action was, the Ehrich brothers had this building erected alongside the Sixth Avenue Elevated and on the 23rd St. horsecar line, which stimulated retail shopping there. When they could not acquire the cast-iron building on the adjoining corner at Sixth Avenue and 23rd St. (see next page), they enlarged their building in an L-shape around it. Thus, they had entrances on both Sixth Avenue and 23rd St. in matching cast-iron facades.

The architectural firm of Alfred Zucker & Co. filed plans for this building in 1886, but while its clients, the Ehrich brothers, were trying to assemble the building site, the building law was changed and the plans had to be altered, especially with respect to fireproofing. However, once construction had started, the fact that this $300,000 building could be completed in six months was a tribute to the efficiency of prefabricated cast-iron parts. Zucker used Renaissance motifs as different as night and day from the design he was readying at the same time for the Durst Building on Lafayette St. (p. 94). In the view of the top story (opposite, top) can be discerned, thanks to the telephoto lens, the monogram "EB," for Ehrich Brothers, and the florid brackets and row of lion's heads along the cornice.

Ehrich Brothers bought up stocks of bankrupt stores and staged highly advertised bargain sales. This style of merchandising seemed to have succeeded, for by 1909 the store had expanded south to 22nd St., its Sixth Avenue frontage extended with a brick and stucco facade designed and painted to look like the adjoining cast-iron front! After all this publicity, success and expansion, however, the Ehrichs, victims of the uptown surge, closed their doors shortly before World War I.

Today the whole thing is still there to be seen. The ground floor has been altered beyond interest. The top four stories with their bold overhanging cornice can best be studied from across Sixth Avenue. The building is well worth a new coat of paint.

112

Right: RIKER'S, 100 WEST 23 ST. (1871, Theodore Trebit). This once sought-after corner, in what was in the 1890s the city's major shopping district, holds a five-story cast-iron building erected in 1871 for a jewelry company. Before the modernizations of recent years, it was distinguished by an incredible cornice full of finials and baroque curves. The small corner structure was able to hold its own when the Ehrich brothers built their big store on both sides of it and tried to absorb it. It still was a great business corner when William B. Riker moved his drugstore into it in 1897. Within a decade this store had become the anchor of a drugstore chain later known as Liggett's.

In our times the building has suffered vicissitudes. One midnight late in 1969, a fire, starting in a wig shop on the second floor, made a torch of the whole edifice. When it was over the ruined tin cornice hung dangerously over the sidewalk and had to be removed, but the two iron facades, though blackened, stood intact. By 1970 the building was rehabilitated, had a new type of aluminum windows and was painted white. Alas, in less than a year a second fire occurred, and again the building survived to be rehabilitated. Who says that cast-iron fronts can't withstand fire?

167 & 169 WEST 23 ST. (altered 1898, P. F. Brohran). Two confections on West 23rd St. that must be seen to be believed. They stand on the north side between Sixth and Seventh Avenues in what was once the theatrical district. Having originally been built as two small residences, they antedated the theaters, which themselves have disappeared. In an 1898 alteration, they were covered with cast-iron fronts to turn them into stores and offices. The exuberant cornices, so large for such little buildings, are of pressed sheet metal. The detail photo shows the fancy little pressed-metal tower of number 167. The elaborate design, tall peaked roof and wrought-iron finial would do justice to a minor skyscraper. One wonders if there is a secret room behind the pedimented dormer window.

Detail of number 169—a glory in pressed metal. When new and painted, pressed metal often cannot be distinguished from cast iron, but here the dent in the top of the pediment is a dead give-away, for cast iron would not dent. The pilasters and window surrounds of cast iron are still in good shape, as is the dainty wrought-iron balcony.

OLD HORNER'S FURNITURE STORE, 61–65 WEST 23 ST. (1886, John B. Snook). In 1887 Robert J. Horner opened a furniture business in this brand new cast-iron building on West 23rd St. John B. Snook, a popular and successful architect, had designed it for Martha Wysong on the site of the Wysong home. In 1895 the Flint Furniture Company took up occupancy nearby; in 1910 the two furniture stores combined; in 1912 Flint and Horner moved to West 36th St.; in 1954 they moved to Long Island.

Snook's design, with its grid of big square-headed windows, afforded bright showrooms for the house furnishings. Photographs made at the turn of the century show Horner's furniture store painted white with the cornices and capitals of the columns in contrasting dark paint. Great striped awnings hung over a sidewalk broader than today's. In the fall of 1971 this building was given a fresh coat of creamy white paint.

116

OLD BEST'S STORE, 60–62 WEST 23 ST. (1905, John B. Snook & Sons). In about 1882, Best & Company moved around the corner from Sixth Avenue into what had been a residence on West 23rd St. Soon it took over the residence next door, too. In 1905 the noted architectural firm of John B. Snook & Sons enlarged and modernized the houses by adding an extra floor, by building onto the rear through to 22nd St., and, most important to our story, by putting a stylish new iron facade on the 23rd St. frontage. A very pleasing metal facade it is, with a central pediment in which it is possible, in a certain light, to discern the word "Best's," long since painted out. At some point the first floor was totally changed to accommodate the Schrafft's restaurant, which occupied it for over half a century. Recently, the building changed hands, and the new owner, developer Jack Resnick, decided to tear it down and replace it with a parking garage despite strong community opposition.

OLD STERN'S DEPARTMENT STORE (32–36 WEST 23 ST., 1878, Henry Fernbach; 38–46 West 23 ST., 1892, William Schickel). One of the largest cast-iron facades in all New York is that of the old Stern's Department Store on West 23rd St. Its present occupant, the New York Merchandise Company, which is to be commended for its exemplary maintenance of the building, has restored it to the creamy white color chosen originally by the Stern brothers and their architects. In 1878 Henry Fernbach, who did many cast-iron commercial buildings farther downtown, created a resplendent emporium for the Stern family on this burgeoning retail shopping block. There was a three-story arch to signalize the doorway and the name "Stern Brothers" was cast in iron on a cornice with volutes and urns. In the next decade West 23rd St. and Stern's prospered together. In 1892 William Schickel, architect of St. Vincent's Hospital in Greenwich Village, was commissioned by the family to enlarge the store. He used duplicate iron castings to expand it westward across an additional five city lots, removed Fernbach's

arched doorway and created his own grand entrance in a new center bay. The J. B. and J. M. Cornell foundry label appears twice on this facade.

The woodcut opposite, made when Stern's was at its zenith sometime after 1892 and before the horseless carriage became prevalent, depicts the building before it had lost its roof cornice decoration and some of the upper story on the east end. The Stern brothers were called "New York's first merchandising family." Besides the four brothers—Louis, Isaac, Bernard and Benjamin—three sisters are also said to have worked in the store. The Sterns knew every customer by name, and people stepping from their carriages felt a personal treatment that began with the doorman's greeting. The first floor of architect Schickel's Renaissance facade, across the frontage of eight city lots, holds special interest for us today because it has escaped "modernization." Bordering large expanses of glass show windows, there are fluted pilasters and the slenderest three-quarter-round attached colonnettes with a design of ivy leaves entwining their upper parts. A series of address numerals cast into round medallions are applied to the columns.

OLD McCUTCHEON'S LINEN STORE, 14 WEST 23 ST. (1882, Henry J. Hardenbergh; 1892, George H. Billings). Three famous New Yorkers are, surprisingly enough, connected with this very prim cast-iron building, actually a done-over Italianate mansion, at center right in the picture. Here Edith Wharton, novelist daughter of wealthy George Frederick Jones, was born in 1862, and here she spent her own age of innocence. After Jones' death in 1882, Henry J. Hardenbergh, celebrated architect of the pres-ent Plaza Hotel and the Dakota Apartments (see p. 177), converted the mansion into a "store with gentlemen's apartments" above. 10 years later, when the neighborhood had changed completely from stylish residential to stylish retail, the building was updated by the addition of an entire cast-iron front. At that time the successful linen merchant James Mc-Cutcheon moved his store from 10 East 14th St. into this building. McCutcheon's, which sup-plied wealthy Americans everywhere with the highest quality of household linens, continues to this day in collaboration with Hammacher Schlemmer on East 57th St. The iron front which we see here, covering Mrs. Wharton's girlhood home, was recently painted a bright medium blue, while the building to its left in the photograph is a chocolate brown. In passing it might be noted that next door at 12 West 23rd St. took place the sensational, never-solved murder of Benjamin Nathan, venerable banker and philanthropist.

214 EAST 34 ST. (1869, William McNamara). As motorists emerge from the 34th St. Manhattan exit of the Queens Midtown Tunnel, they find themselves face to face with a memorable cast-iron building. Peck & Hills, the furniture company that now occupies it, has given it an arresting charcoal-gray and white paint job. In 1869 John Glass, the owner-builder, employed architect William McNamara to design a building as a market hall with meeting rooms above. For a while the new "Glass Hall" had a police gymnasium on one upper floor, and, by 1880, Dr. John A. Wyeth's medical classes on another. By 1884 Dr. Wyeth's fledgling Polyclinic Medical School pioneered in providing free local clinics where young physicians could gain experience with patients. A hospital section was established in 1888, which soon expanded into the building next door as the Polyclinic Medical School and Hospital. In 1896 a fire, which started in an adjacent factory, all but wiped out the hospital, but the ornate cast-iron front stood firm and strong after the blaze. The entire structure was restored behind it, with a new story added. Polyclinic Hospital occupied this building until 1912, when it moved to the West Side.

MOUNT MORRIS FIRE WATCHTOWER (c. 1855, James Bogardus?). Probably James Bogardus, self-styled "originator and constructor of iron buildings," erected this skeletal cast-iron fire lookout tower for the city. It stands on the tall rocky outcropping in Mount Morris Park at the northernmost end of Fifth Avenue. From his great height in the little cupola on the four-story tower, the watchman gazed across the roofs of Harlem, striking the bell to signal to local fire companies when he spotted a fire.

Bogardus had used this same post-and-lintel type of construction earlier in octagonal iron fire towers, one at 33rd St. and Ninth Avenue built in 1851, and another on Spring St. between Varick and Macdougal Sts. built in 1853. After the city was divided into eight fire districts in 1850, Bogardus urged that his new cast-iron constructions be utilized instead of wooden towers. This was very timely, for already several timber belltowers had gone up in flames.

The slender iron columns of the fire tower are delicately fluted, and the sweep of the staircase spiraling up around the bell creates a lacy silhouette against the sky. The Mount Morris Fire Tower is, in the 1970's, an unexpected souvenir, and has been officially designated as a city landmark.

Opposite: BRIDLE PATH ARCH IN CENTRAL PARK (1869, Calvert Vaux). In its early days Central Park contained several examples of cast-iron park architecture. These included summer houses, a bandstand and bridges, most of which have been allowed to disintegrate. A private group, the Friends of Central Park, is striving to have the fragile cast-iron Ladies' Pavilion restored and also has found two generous Friends, Lucy G. Moss and Lila Acheson Wallace, who will provide the large sum necessary for the Parks Department to restore the famed iron Bow Bridge in the southern part of the park. Less known, only because it is in a less frequented section of the park, is the cast-iron Bridle Path Arch shown in our photograph. It is a footbridge north of the 96th St. transverse. The beautiful flowing design is the work of Calvert Vaux, architect-collaborator with landscape architect Frederick Law Olmsted in the creation of Central Park. The Bridle Path Arch needs paint, but it needs more than that. So the Friends of Central Park have commissioned a study of the arch to be underwritten by a special Friend, Arthur Ross.

Above: IRONCLAD BANK, CORNER OF FULTON & FRONT STS., BROOKLYN (1868). One of the few remaining iron buildings in Brooklyn, the Ironclad Bank originally housed the Long Island Safety Deposit Company, and stood on the then-busy Fulton St., close to the ferry to Fulton St. in Manhattan. From 1869 to 1883, Brooklyn Bridge was erected over the head of this modest two-story Italian palazzo. The building has three arched bays on Fulton St. and three more around the corner on Front St. There is an arched doorway in the chamfered corner of its facade. Its cornice and roof-line balustrade are gone. Inside, a tall central iron column supports the second floor, and a bold freestanding iron staircase leads to it. The bank stood empty for nearly 30 years, until a local group leased it in 1969 for use as a cultural center.This group appears to have lost out and the building is being painted black by its present owner. The whole area may soon get a new lease on life through zoning changes projected by the City Planning Commission.

287 BROADWAY (1871, John B. Snook). John B. Snook, best known for his design for the first Grand Central Station, was commissioned a century ago by the Storm family to build a prestige office building (to house lawyers' chambers and a bank) on part of the site of that famous old hotel, the Irving House. The Irving had been quite a fashionable hostelry, whose guests included such celebrities as Jenny Lind.

The mansard roof with dormers, providing a sixth floor and giving 287 Broadway its French Second Empire look, was added some time after the original cast-iron building had been completed. An early Otis elevator serviced all six floors. That typical lacy iron cresting along the top of the roof, which has been lost totally or in part from most mansard roofs, fortunately is intact here.

A high stoop led to a grand main floor over a high basement containing shops. The stoop was removed in 1912, but the dignified doorway can be made out in the photograph opposite behind the circular sign of Sun Cosmetics. Think what an impressive banking room that main floor provided behind its long range of very tall arched windows. Indeed, throughout the building the windows, which are arched and have keystones, are extremely large, extending almost from floor to ceiling. In 287 Broadway we see the rhythmic repetition of identical parts exemplifying the use of cast iron in an efficient and economical way to create architecture of considerable grandeur. The iron for this handsome building was cast in the foundry of Jackson, Burnet & Company, according to the architect's account books. This building and the now city-owned 1846 marble A. T. Stewart store across the street (often referred to as the Sun Building because it was occupied for a third of a century by the *New York Sun* newspaper) are both true landmarks of the City Hall area and should receive official designation and protection at once.

"THOMAS TWINS": 317 BROADWAY (above & opposite left, demolished) & 319 BROADWAY (opposite right, still standing; both 1869, David & John Jardine). 317 Broadway, like its identical twin at 319 Broadway, was originally an office building. Each had a steep stoop leading to the main floor set on a high basement. Each had a frontage of 25 feet on Broadway and a range 15 windows in length stretching down Thomas St. This range was punctuated by

strong flat piers, dividing it into bays of five windows each. The buildings presented the purest of iron architecture, using the material molded into countless identical parts to create endless rows of identical arched windows between endless rows of identical columns. In the photo above, 317 is shown before its demolition had begun; in the photo opposite left, during demolition.

In December 1971, almost exactly a hun-

dred years after it had been completed for General Thomas A. Davies, Civil War hero and Croton Aqueduct engineer, 317, the Thomas Twin on the southwest corner of Broadway and Thomas St., was torn down. The city's Landmarks Preservation Commission had held the requisite public hearings, yet failed to take action that would have helped protect the building. The demolition of this classic iron building dismayed the growing number of ad-

mirers of cast iron who came to dicker with the demolition foreman for beautiful acanthus-leaf capitals, for scrolled keystones and even for the D. D. Badger foundry mark. This was bolted to the farthermost column on the Thomas St. side and evidenced that the Architectural Iron Works had cast the many parts for this great iron building.

The remaining "Thomas Twin" (right) still stands on the northwest corner of Broadway and Thomas St., a hundred years separating it from the overpowering telephone skyscraper being built behind it. The five stories of Italianate architecture, once painted white, are dirty and flawed by a fire escape and blatant signs for the lunchrooms and stores. They originally housed professional offices above, while railroad ticket agencies occupied the daylight basement area. The Broadway scene was much enhanced when the identical "Thomas Twin" flanked the entrance to narrow Thomas St., a private right-of-way that harks back to the days when it was the carriage drive into the grounds of the New York Hospital. The hospital was begun in September 1773, and demolished in May 1869, after which Thomas St. was cut through the grounds to Broadway. The remaining Twin should have official landmark protection.

361 BROADWAY (1881, W. Wheeler Smith). This is a monumental cast-iron office building on the southwest corner of Broadway and Franklin St. Its six-window-wide Broadway frontage is repeated three times in the length westward along Franklin St. The entire surface is strongly modeled with distinct cornice lines at each floor level, while strong vertical lines created by free-standing columns create deep window reveals. It gives a powerful impression of squareness, as in the square piers at the corners, the broad square-headed windows and the level, squared-off roof cornice with a central pediment, itself perched on a square decorative panel. The large sheets of glass in the double-hung sash of the windows indicate the extent to which American glass technology had developed by 1880. The awe-inspiring colonnade of the Franklin St. facade, as well as most of the Broadway facade, stands as it was built, with very little "modernizing." In the early 1800s this was a residential area. Directly across the street, David Clarkson, whose wife was a member of the wealthy De Peyster family, had a two-story home set in a garden that embraced the whole block. He sold the land to Rufus King, who in 1808 divided it into lots. Residential buildings were soon turned to commercial use, and we know that before the Civil War Mathew Brady opened his second photographic studio over a saloon at 359 Broadway.

So inventive was architect W. Wheeler Smith that a careful scrutiny of the six floors of this building, of which the upper five appear in the photo opposite, reveals different details at each floor level. Take along your opera glasses and you will find that this is true of corner piers as well as of the unusual decoration of the columns and their capitals. While the second, fourth and fifth-floor columns have vine-like spiral designs, the third and sixth-floor columns have a geometric fluted and banding design. For some years, Munn & Co. published *Scientific American* in the upper floors. Albert G. Hyde & Co., converters of cotton goods, were identified with this building from late in the 19th century until after World War I. Subsequently, a tool and hardware jobber took the ground floor and only recently vacated it for more space on Long Island. The building's owners, A. Gindoff & Co., appreciate its good looks, paint it every five years, and are distressed by damage suffered by the iron column pedestals from heavy trucks in the process of loading. Upper floors contain a greeting card firm and a manufacturer of sheets and pillowcases.

Further details are illustrated on the next two pages.

The stunning tall cast-iron columns along the Broadway facade of 361 Broadway (opposite) stand on yard-high cast-iron pedestals. Wheeler Smith, the architect, banded them with a line of guilloche pattern about one third up their height, then twined about the lower shaft a pliant branch with leaves and berries. The same beautiful treatment appears on the 16 columns lining the Franklin St. facade. He was working on a new building for Sloane's big carpet store at 888 Broadway at the same time, and there again can be seen leaf-entwined columns, especially along its 19th St. side (p. 173). Many of the iron-front buildings with their large glazed openings were provided with rolling iron shutters to be pulled down at night. Here at 361 Broadway you can observe the iron shutters pushed virtually out of sight at the tops of the windows. Probably they are rusted into position, but they originally rode up and down in the channel slits to be found on either side of each window, totally hidden by the grand columns.

Several square piers run the entire height of the building on its Franklin St. facade, dividing it into three bays. They sustain an enormous weight from floors and roof. Similar piers occur at each corner of the building. The decorative exterior cladding of the hidden structural members takes the form of cast-iron pilasters with stylized capitals (right). The pilasters have a recessed central panel within which appears a design of the same leafy branch with berries that is wound about so many of the columns on the two facades of the building.

GROSVENOR BUILDING, 385 BROADWAY (1875, Charles Wright). A solid, business-like Victorian structure built for Matilda Grosvenor and Charlotte Goodridge a hundred years ago on the west side of Broadway, south of Canal St. Presumably it was a real-estate investment, a building suitable to the dry-goods trade that flourished in this area. A smaller Grosvenor Building, built in 1869, already stood around the corner west of Broadway at 64 White St. The pediments of both buildings bear the name "Grosvenor" and the dates of erection. The architect has given character to the Broadway building by placing three-quarter-round unadorned columns on either side of windows with the flat tops and rounded corners set within deep reveals. The emphasis is on structure rather than decoration. The latter is at a minimum, yet early photographs do show that at the top of the cornice stood a half dozen cast-iron urns.

The building has been owned for the last 15 years by J. Roffman, who says he has it painted every four or five years, always with two coats of paint. A firm dealing in rayons has used the ground-floor space for over 25 years.

427–429 BROADWAY (1870, Thomas R. Jackson) & 425 BROADWAY (1869, Griffith Thomas). Two early dry-goods stores can be seen in this view of Broadway, and a third down Howard St. where it ends at Mercer St. At the corner stands 427–429, an extremely handsome palazzo of cast iron with two shining facades, row piled upon row of arched windows, and a well-proportioned cornice held on brackets. In the pediment on the front elevation is the date 1870, the year in which this store was built for A. J. Dittenhofer. On the left, at 425 Broadway, hung with fire escapes, is the five-story iron-front building with a broken pediment built for Le Boutillier Brothers, a New York merchandising family prominent into the mid-20th century. Then, down the block on the southeast corner of Howard and Mercer Sts., is glimpsed the rear of Arnold Constable's store (1857, Griffith Thomas). The rear, of course, is brick with arched windows and cornice over a first floor of cast iron. Its marble front is still to be seen facing on Canal St. A study in foundry labels can be made here, for Le Boutillier's carries the trademark of Excelsior Iron Works, Dittenhofer's that of Aetna Iron Works, while the iron work on Arnold Constable's is marked Merklee & Nichol.

444 BROADWAY (left & opposite left) & 452 BROADWAY (opposite right; both 1876, August Schweitzer & Emile Gruwe). In Britain, where engineers made earlier use of cast iron than did architects, some beautiful and enduring utilitarian results were achieved. For example, cast-iron bridges were produced, such as the beautiful 1779 high-arched iron bridge at Coalbrookdale and the 1814 iron Craigellachie Bridge by Thomas Telford. Great glass and iron train sheds were suspended over railroad station platforms. Sweeping greenhouses and market halls and, above all, the fabulous Crystal Palace were created, all of glass held in slender wood and iron supports. Primarily, the iron was employed for its strength and lightness. Interstices were filled with glass.

In 1876 two New York engineers, August Schweitzer and Emile Gruwe, built the light, open, lacy iron fronts shown in our pictures. They look very different from what architects were putting up adjacent to them and also on the other side of Broadway, buildings composed in a more traditional way, their elements copied directly from stone prototypes. The two buildings are 75 feet apart. As the more southerly one at 444 Broadway has been painted a buff color—with its colonnettes and leafy filigree a blue-green—it is by far the more attractive. However, a long look at number 452—with its dirty, dark red paint—will disclose that they are identical twins. These 25-foot facades are just about as flat as they can be. At each level, the three-abreast windows, nearly seven feet across, are separated by attenuated columns with meagre decoration. Most appealing of all are the filigree arches which overlay the tops of the square-headed windows, showing a perforated leaf-and-vine design that suggests Art Nouveau. A foundry label on 452 Broadway quite uniquely bears the designers' names, Schweitzer and Gruwe, as well as the words "Long Island Iron Works, Brooklyn." What cannot be known from looking at the Broadway frontage is that these buildings come together in the rear at 10–16 Crosby St., forming a "U" around and behind the big 75-foot cast-iron building that stands between them. This 75-foot iron front stretching across numbers 446, 448 and 450 went up also in 1876. John B. Snook designed it for the Lorillard estate, and J. B. & J. M. Cornell manufactured the iron castings.

444 Broadway stands on the east side of the street, just north of Howard St., on what was a very lively block in the early decades of the 19th century. Lorillard's circus performed here around 1810. As the real estate became too valuable for circus use, Tattersall's famed livery

stable, riding school and very large horse market took over part of the circus land, and the Olympic Theatre occupied other parts. The Olympic Theatre, which nearly failed at first, was rescued by William Mitchell, and thanks to his policy of low prices and satires on "local incidents and prevailing follies," by 1846 became "the most popular theatre in New York." The City Assembly Rooms, the best known ballrooms in the City, were developed here in 1853. By the beginning of 1876, the block had turned to trade with little left from the old days, except the Olympic Theatre, transformed by this time into the Hotel Continental. Then a terrific fire swept the block at the rush hour on the evening of February 9. Great crowds gathered as they left work in the vicinity, and proved hard to control. The fire started at 10 Crosby St. in a trimmings and feathers shop. The flames spread through the block to Broadway, swirling around numbers 444 and 446. After the conflagration had raged for more than an hour, "the roof of 444 and 446 fell in, forcing out the walls. Soon the walls of 448 and 450 fell into Broadway." Apparently, the first-floor store fronts of cast iron were thrown to the pavement and "Broadway was strewn with huge pieces of iron fronts that had fallen when forced down by the falling roofs and walls from above" (*New York Times*, Feb. 9, 1876, p. 1). As for lot number 444, this was its fourth bad fire. The present building, with its twin at 452 Broadway, was put up later that year.

462 BROADWAY (1879, John Correja). This big iron double building at 462–468 Broadway, on the northeast corner of Grand St., was built for George Bliss, an attorney, and Frederick H. Cossitt, a merchant, who leased it at once to the great wholesale firm of Mills & Gibb. These importers of fine laces and linens were here until World War I. Recent decades have seen number 462 occupied by firms handling Venetian blinds, leatherette and plastic sheeting.

In its northern portion the floors originally encircled a light court illuminated by a large overhead skylight. But as artificial lighting improved, all floors were filled in within the inner court area. This alteration seems to have been poorly done, for on January 27, 1966, the central area of the fifth floor collapsed, overloaded by great rolls of plastic sheeting. Floor after floor beneath gave way under the weight like a stack of cards. Fortunately, employees were out on coffee break, and no one was seriously injured. The exterior iron structure stood straight as a die when the present owners purchased 462 Broadway with half of its interior looking like a pile of jackstraws. Within months enormous steel beams were put in to support new floors. In the end it was practically a new structure, but the cast-iron exterior required no attention beyond a coat of fresh paint.

The five-story cast-iron building to the right of 462 Broadway in the picture opposite is 134–136 Grand St. (1871), which startles everyone who glances at it. The immediate feeling is that here is a building which has been scalped, as indeed it has. Early pictures show it with a tall mansard roof of slate, the tower at each corner marked by elaborate dormer windows sprouting urns and finials. The topmost element, a square pedimented cupola bearing the date 1871, still remains, but all the rest is gone, including highly ornamented bull's-eye dormers, five on each side. What a cruel alteration!

ROOSEVELT BUILDING, 478–482 BROADWAY (1874, Richard Morris Hunt). The great Richard Morris Hunt, America's first Parisian-trained architect, known for his mansions for millionaires, not to mention the Metropolitan Museum and the base of the Statue of Liberty, designed two commercial buildings with cast-iron fronts. These were no run-of-the-mill structures. The one which was long ago demolished displayed a Moorish design, and this existing one, often called Neo-Grec in style, is also highly individual in character. Montgomery Schuyler wrote in 1895, "The 'iron age' in commercial building produced nothing better than these two fronts and very few things so good."

Designing with iron for iron's sake, Hunt broke away from the customary imitation of stone. He raised four giant columns, laced them together with arches of filigree, and suspended behind them what was essentially a curtain wall of glass. The building has an extension eastward through the block to narrow Crosby St., where to one's surprise number 40 appears as a quite beautiful echo of the center of this Broadway facade (see p. 87).

The five floors of 478 Broadway have simple rectangular windows divided by the slenderest of columns and grouped into three wide bays demarcated by fluted pilasters on the ground floor becoming giant fluted Ionic columns above, which are connected by delicate tracery spanning the fourth-floor windows. The fifth story is integrated into the design by a cornice with an outward sweep reminiscent of some Egyptian temples. Now stripped bare, the cavetto cornice until recent times carried its original metal edging in perforated tracery design. We are fortunate that this building, erected by a master, has survived much as he conceived it, with even the ground floor largely intact.

The emphatically modeled Neo-Grec ground-

floor pilasters (see detail photo) each carry a circular shield—cast separately and bolted to the building's surface—bearing the numerals of the address. The question often arises as to why this building carries the name of Roosevelt. The answer is that it was built as an investment by Roosevelt Hospital, which had inherited the site by the will of its founder and benefactor James H. Roosevelt, who from 1843 to 1861 had had both his law office and his residence here. Never having married, he left his entire estate—much of it in real estate—for the establishment of the hospital to serve the city of New York.

503–511 BROADWAY (1878, John B. Snook).
These three big, iron-front buildings intended
to look like a single structure were put up for
the Loubats, a father and son who spent most
of their time in France, from designs by architect John B. Snook. The impressive proportions of the four stories of colonnades, one
atop the other, are communicated in this rak-
ing shot looking south along Broadway. There
is a classic austerity about the 48 identical
iron columns, whose slightly belled capitals
have been stripped of their acanthus leaves
(bolt holes can still be discerned). The iron
was cast in the huge Cornell Foundry. The
younger Loubat made large gifts to the Catho-
lic Church for which Pope Leo XIII gave him
the title Duke. Loubat donated these buildings
to Columbia University in exchange for an an-
nuity of $60,000 which he drew until his death
in 1927 at the age of 96, giving him the best of
the bargain. Sad to tell, the buildings, whose
huge lofts run 200 feet through to Mercer
Street and are used for light manufacturing,
are sadly abused, their double hung windows
streaked with grime and marred by torn window shades.

Fortunately the decorative cornice is still
well preserved. Such is not the case in many
other buildings. When repairs to cornices call
for a monetary outlay, the cornices are too
often summarily pulled off. The Buildings Department of the City of New York is to be commended for a recent directive to its building
inspectors urging them to encourage owners
to repair existing cornices rather than remove
them. Mindless removal of cornices violates
the integrity of the design of most 19th-cen-
tury commercial buildings.

537–541 BROADWAY (1868, Charles Mettam). These two buildings, erected on three city lots between Prince and Spring Sts., stand in what was once a colorful hotel and theater district. They have strong five-story facades with great expanses of glass windows under almost flattened arches springing from smooth three-quarter-round columns with composite capitals. It is true to cast iron, this very open fenestration, this repetitious use of prefabricated identical units. Even the decoration is repetitive, cast in a single mold: for example, the 21 circular medallions that appear in the spandrels above the columns, and the classical balustrade beneath each second-floor window. This identical precast balustrade element once stretched across the entire first floor.

Years of changing the big advertising signs which firms used to hang on the fronts of the buildings have apparently taken their toll of half of the balustrade. There is a strong cornice line at every floor, while the roof cornice has arched pediments with urns balanced on either side and a triangular central pediment topped by another urn. The treatment of the roof, and of the original trabeated ground-floor arcade of tall, free-standing columns, served to unify the design of the two buildings, and make them appear as one. However, the fact that today one is kept better painted than the other betrays their separate ownership.

Charles Mettam designed them shortly after the Civil War for joint owners Benjamin Franklin Beekman, who had his office here, and Peter Gilsey, the strong advocate of cast iron, who was soon to build the big cast-iron Gilsey Hotel, still standing on Broadway at 29th St. (p. 166). These Broadway buildings were later extended the full 200 feet through the block to Mercer St., where they appear as numbers 108–112 Mercer. There was a fire in the buildings about 15 years after they were built, but the damage was soon repaired. The altering of the first floors —to enclose the free-standing colonnade within the display windows, thus creating more floor space for the stores within—was done in 1942.

Above: The mansard roof added to the Rouss Building in 1900 is finished at each end by a tower with pyramidal decor. Paired square pillars rise from a balustrade to support a broken pediment surmounted by a grimacing lion's face. The pyramidal towers decorate both the cast-iron front on Broadway and the brick rear building. Behind the mansard roof Rouss had a well-appointed, wood-paneled penthouse, which he frequently occupied. Small manufacturing firms, especially dress and garment makers, now predominate in this handsomely maintained building.

Opposite: LITTLE SINGER BUILDING, 561–563 BROADWAY (1904, Ernest Flagg). In 1908 the Singer Sewing Machine Company employed Ernest Flagg to create its trademark Singer Building, for a while the world's tallest building, downtown at Broadway and Liberty St.

Earlier it had commissioned him to do this smaller L-shaped 12-story office and loft building on Broadway near Prince St. Departing from his own precedents, Flagg designed an innovative colored terra-cotta, glass and steel structure that to this day wins the admiration of all who see it and certainly foretells the glass curtain wall. The delicate balconies and the tracery framing the great arch near its top are of wrought iron, not cast iron. It has a Broadway frontage of 50 feet and wraps around the old marble corner edifice (formerly Ball Black's jewelry store) to 88 Prince St., where a second frontage of 37 feet echoes the Broadway facade. Shortly after the Civil War the Singer Company had a factory on Mott St. that was, according to D. D. Badger, "perfectly fireproof," having been built almost entirely of iron. It is depicted in Plate IV in his 1865 catalogue, *Illustrations of Iron Architecture*.

Above: 628–630 BROADWAY (1882, Herman J. Schwarzmann). The Philadelphia architect Herman J. Schwarzmann was in charge of the overall layout of that city's great Centennial Exhibition of 1876, for which he designed monumental Memorial Hall, as well as 33 other structures. By putting his imprint on the trendsetting fair, he influenced American architecture in general. He brought the playful spirit of exhibition architecture to a workaday office building on Broadway when he created this charming iron front for Henry Newman's New York Mercantile Exchange. No imitation of stone here: floral and natural motifs give surface interest to a nearly flat facade that is almost all glass. Engaged colonnettes between the windows simulate slender bamboo poles, while flowers wreathe up the more solid center column and graceful bouquets of lilies decorate the second floor. Oriental filigree arches cap the windows of the top story, above which runs a frieze of leaves beneath the bracketed galvanized iron cornice, which once carried a very lacy cresting.

Opposite: 648 BROADWAY (1891, Cleverdon & Putzel; 1898 addition, Robert T. Lyons). Some people forget that cast iron was being used for architectural purposes through the 1890s. There are several examples in this book, and here is another. It was put up in 1891 as an eight-story structure, quite tall as cast-iron fronts go, and cost $185,000. Then, in 1898, looking like an afterthought, an additional two stories were added to provide store lofts and sample rooms. The facade is actually one large central panel of iron and glass, with only the side piers of brick. Judging from this view taken with a telephoto lens, the supports of those top two stories are lengths of cast-iron pipe sheathed in pressed metal grooved into a spiral design. Ionic volutes are fastened to the pipes near the spring of the window arches. Glancing below to the original eight-story portion, we find between the windows narrow supports with delicate decoration. They sustain broad, horizontal members with telltale nails that once held advertising signs. The arcade of small arched windows with wreaths in their spandrels is rather pretty, but all the detail seems too small for the height at which it is placed. When architects expanded or heightened existing iron fronts by the use of matching castings, more consistent results were achieved than here. We have seen this use of matching castings, for instance, in the former Rouss store at 555 Broadway, in the Bennett Building on Nassau St. (p. 5) and in Altman's store (p. 105) and Stern's store (p. 119) in the old 23rd St. shopping area. Today 648 Broadway is a hive of light industry: ladies' apparel, sportswear, belts, handbags, threads, men's hats, paper bags and printed cards. The ground floor has recently been painted a dark green, but the upper floors have a dusty cocoa look about them. Beside the rather elaborate doorway can be seen the foundry label of J. B. & J. M. Cornell.

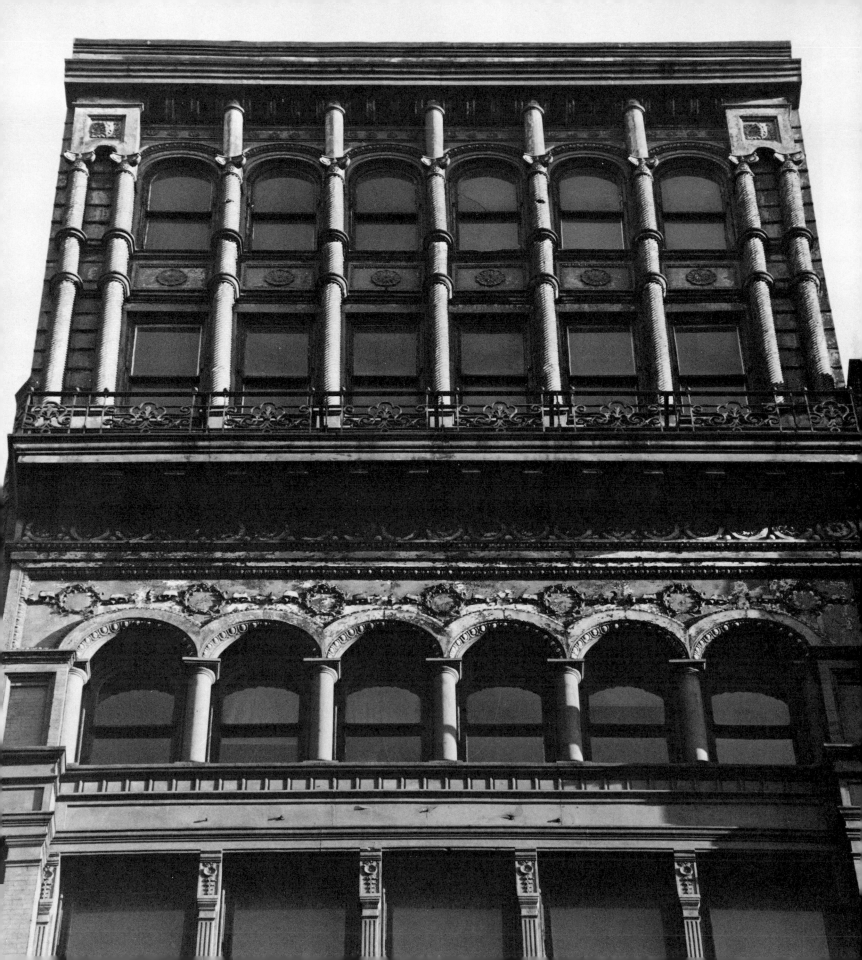

Sometime after that, a spectacular crowning decor with urns was removed from the center of the roof cornice. The Jardines' stylish building is presently occupied by firms that do leather tanning and converting. Opposite stands the once flamboyant Broadway Central Hotel, the southern portion of which suffered a tragic collapse in August 1973 following interior structural changes.

Opposite: 687–691 BROADWAY (1884 & 1887, J. A. Wood). This is a building that does not try to masquerade as stone but flaunts its cast-iron front. The delicate free-standing colonnettes, which could not possibly be of stone, make the strips of windows look almost like loggias. Although the camera's eye discerns the essential unity of the design, in fact the section on the right is maintained as a separate building. This is apparent from its different color and its fresher paint, also from its fire escape and its commercially altered first floor. By contrast, the section on the left seems to have had indifferent maintenance, for it is a dingy chocolate brown and has lost some of its decorative iron details. Nonetheless, the fact that it lacks a fire escape and has had no alteration of the first floor enables the viewer to reconstruct its original aspect in his imagination. For this, however, the whole lost roof decor must be replaced in the mind's eye: a balustrade right across the roof line with pedestals at each end holding pointed finials, also a central pediment tipped with acroteria and displaying the date 1887 beneath a sunburst design.

Old City Building Department records indicate that the section on the right was built in 1884 for Mr. Albert Tower at a cost of $90,000. The records show, too, that the section on the left, which has an extra bay with a major entrance on the ground floor, was built three years later for the same Mr. Tower by the same architect, J. A. Wood, but at a cost of $110,000. Both parts of the building were designed as stores. When cast-iron buildings were at the height of their popularity, the broad architrave of the cornice at each floor served a utilitarian purpose, for long strip signs, the breadth of the structure, were fastened into each cornice. The large raised gold lettering, characteristic of the period, took its place quite comfortably in the building's overall design. A 19th-century photograph depicts the left section of this building painted white and bearing several large strip signs. The Jefferson Screw Corp. now occupies number 691 in its entirety, while number 687 houses diversified light manufacturing, including belt-buckle assembling and production of fireplace equipment.

Above: 678 BROADWAY (1874, David & John Jardine). When Walt Whitman wrote in his poem "Mannahatta" of ". . . crowded streets, high growths of iron, slender, strong, light, splendidly uprising toward clear skies," he was surely recalling his strolls up Broadway. Just such a tall cast-iron beauty as this may have stirred his thoughts. It is of unique design.

Very open and glassy, it was done in the French mode by the brothers David and John Jardine for their old client, General Thomas A. Davies. They had already produced the Thomas Twins for him five years earlier (pp. 128 & 129). The ground floor at 678 Broadway once had tall show windows between columns, but all this has been changed since a big alteration in 1898.

OLD A. T. STEWART STORE, BROADWAY BETWEEN 9 & 10 ST. (1862, John Kellum). Probably the largest cast-iron building anywhere ever was the A. T. Stewart department store, shown in this 1906 photograph. It stood on the eastern edge of Greenwich Village for nearly a hundred years, most of them under the ownership of the Wanamakers, who ran this store from 1896 until 1954. Shoppers still recall the great central rotunda with the upper floors rising around it like the galleries in an opera house. They recall, too, the glass skylight, the grand double staircase and the sonorous organ music, especially during the Christmas season. Daringly far uptown in 1862, the store soon became the anchor for the so-called Ladies' Mile of expensive retail establishments. Its design is one of classic simplicity: a trabeated colonnade at the ground floor with vast sheets of plate glass between tall Corinthian columns and, above this, four tiers of 84 identical windows, their seg-mental arches springing from shapely columns. The J. B. and W. W. Cornell foundry made the cast iron, which was painted white, while Peter Cooper's foundry made the wrought-iron beams used with cast-iron columns in the interior. On July 14, 1956, the vacant store, awaiting demolition to make way for the present Stewart Apartment House, was struck by one of the city's worst fires—a fire that burned out of control for a day, consuming all wooden floors and fixtures. According to Alan Burnham, writing in *The Architectural Record* two months later, "the interior system of columns and girders remained straight, as did the cast-iron exterior." The iron had to be knocked down with a wrecker's ball. Only then, Burnham wrote, was it revealed "that continuous vertical columns transmitted the loads from the topmost floor directly to the foundation . . . and in this lay the seeds of the sky-scraper."

after giving up the 11th St. store, they opened a larger one at 5 West 34th St. But by World War I, they had to close the 23rd St. store, and by 1954 they were out of business entirely.

When John Kellum designed the iron building for Lake and McCreery, he crowned it with a splendid mansard roof which, with its lacy cresting, has long since been replaced by a low fifth story with square windows. The iron was fabricated and put up by the outstanding firm of J. B. and W. W. Cornell. A search for an iron founder's mark has been fruitless, although one would think that the manufacturer would be proud to put his name on this imposing store.

801 Broadway looks across to old Grace Church and, for years after McCreery's left, was occupied by a ladies' shoe and handbag factory and an antique statuary store. Early on the morning of October 31, 1971, a fire which could not be controlled for several hours broke out in the factory, and yet the handsome exterior, its 11th St. side looking much as it did a hundred years ago, withstood the blaze. In the spring of 1972, a real estate developer purchased the old McCreery building with its charred interior, intending to replace it with a new apartment structure, but he and his architect, realizing its potential for adaptive use, are now converting it to residential purposes.

The detail photo shows the dramatic colonnade of smooth three-quarter-round engaged columns on paneled pedestals that ennobles the very long 11th St. range of Kellum's Renaissance building. Their Corinthian capitals sustain an entablature with modillions beneath its strongly projecting cornice. This long facade presents one of the most stirring views of cast iron in the city. Endless architecture, every part identical—the best use of cast iron. Resting on the first-floor colonnade are three floors of keystoned arches carried on the Corinthian columns. The first floor is a full 20 feet in height with broad glass windows, through which light flooded the store's sales counters. Upper floors are of decreasing height.

A. T. Stewart's monumental block-square cast-iron palazzo across the street (preceding page), done in 1862 and also by Kellum, may well have led to this architect's receiving the commission for the McCreery Store a few years later. 801 Broadway unquestionably merits designation as a landmark.

OLD McCREERY'S DRY GOODS STORE, 801 BROADWAY (1868, John Kellum). McCreery's Dry Goods Store, shown in the woodcut opposite, from an 1869 issue of *Harper's Weekly*, occupied the fine cast-iron structure at Broadway and 11th St. from 1868 until 1902. Mc-Creery's built it for $300,000, then sold it to the Methodist Book Concern, leasing back the lower floors. The firm did a land-office business here and for a while had a big store constructed for them on the site of the Booth Theater, 23rd St. at Sixth Avenue. Not long

OLD ARNOLD CONSTABLE STORE, 881–887 BROADWAY (1868–1876, Griffith Thomas). The heroic mansard roof is the feature that most often attracts attention to this big Victorian-looking cast-iron building that was once Arnold Constable's dry-goods store at the southeast corner of Fifth Avenue and 19th St. Its main facade, of white marble, was on Broadway at 19th St. The noted architect Griffith Thomas designed it in 1868. Mr. Aaron Arnold thought that marble was the only material suitable for a fine building, and his earlier store, also done in marble by Thomas, can still be seen on the northeast corner of Canal and Mercer Sts. Arnold and his son-in-law James Constable did such a tremendous business in their new Broadway store that they expanded by extending its 19th St. side. Then, to add more floors, the ungainly two-story mansard roof was constructed. Finally, they built all the way to Fifth Avenue and erected there in 1877 an annex for the wholesale departments. Mr. Arnold died at this time, and, interestingly enough, when architect Thomas was called upon to build the Fifth Avenue facade, he recreated the Broadway front, not in marble but in cast iron. It appealed to Constable for reasons of both economy and fire retardation. He continued the dramatic, steep French roof right along 19th St. and around the Fifth Avenue side, where today it is probably the city's largest, most interesting and best-preserved mansard. Arnold Constable's vacated this building when they moved uptown in 1914.

OLD LORD & TAYLOR STORE, 901 BROAD-WAY (1869, James H. Giles). Samuel Lord and George Washington Taylor established a store in 1826 at 47 Catherine St. Slip near the docks of the East River, selecting their dry goods from the cargoes of sailing vessels. In 1853 the firm bought a large coal yard at the corner of Grand and Chrystie Sts., and built a new Lord & Taylor with a spacious central rotunda under a glass dome. In 1860 they built a branch at the northwest corner of Grand and Broadway, and less than a decade later, quick to sense the shift in retail trade, felt they had decided on the ultimate location: Broadway near Madison Square. At the corner of 20th St. they built a cast-iron palace, a French Second Empire extravaganza designed by James H. Giles. It was five stories tall and had a hundred-foot frontage on Broadway marked by an elaborate two-story arched entrance, above which, in the mansard roof, rose a tower, its top rimmed with lacy metal cresting. Sadly, almost that entire frontage is gone today, but not so the tower at the 20th St. corner, which appears in our photograph. It is quite astounding as it is, but when Lord & Taylor held forth as luxury merchants here, this tower was replete with finials, a balustrade, a highly ornamented round dormer window and a crown of cresting, while from its top flagpole streamed a pennant with the name of the store. The store's plush and novel elevators interested everyone. Lord & Taylor, always outstanding for style and quality, weathered the panic of 1873, not long after they opened this store, but at the cost of closing their two downtown establishments. Later, needing more space, they expanded here six times, stretching down 20th St. and around onto Fifth Avenue. Their masonry annex at Fifth Avenue and 20th St. is still there, but most of the cast-iron additions on 20th St. have been pulled down to accommodate parking lots. Lord & Taylor's windows have been famous from the beginning. An 1872 commentator said, "They are always filled with a magnificent display of the finest goods and attract crowds of gazers." They invented the Christmas window featuring fantasy instead of merchandise. Lord & Taylor, along with its next-block neighbor, Arnold Constable, having helped establish the Ladies' Mile around 1870, departed it together in 1914, following the retail trade to Fifth Avenue near 42nd St.

OLD GILSEY HOTEL, 1200 BROADWAY (1869, Stephen D. Hatch). The last farmhouse standing in midtown on Broadway was demolished to make way for the Gilsey Hotel. The old clapboard, hip-roofed, green-shuttered homestead of Caspar Samlar had a long, low front porch, and stood behind trees and a picket fence. When Gilsey acquired the corner in 1868, a row of high-stooped brownstones had already been built to the east of the farmhouse. At the Fifth Avenue corner was the 1854 Marble Collegiate Church, made famous in our time by Dr. Norman Vincent Peale, who married Julie Nixon and David Eisenhower there.

Peter Gilsey was a colorful New Yorker who, like A. T. Stewart, invested deeply in real estate and enthusiastically favored cast iron as a building material. Both recognized the economy of erecting buildings with prefabricated cast-iron sections. Both wanted rich, ornamental effects, and these could be had with iron. Both were progressive men who wanted the latest style, and cast iron was definitely "in." Thus, Stewart had built his big department store on Broadway and 10th St. (p. 160) of iron, and Gilsey had put up a downtown iron office building at Broadway and Cortlandt St. And when Gilsey audaciously decided in 1869

to build an elaborate hotel as far uptown as Madison Square, he again chose cast iron, combining it with some marble, and gloried in the florid French Second Empire design worked out by architect Stephen D. Hatch. Hatch, too, seemed to like the French mode for cast iron, as he used it again in 1870 at 1 Bond St. for D. D. Appleton (p. 88). In 1881 he did the famous Murray Hill Hotel on Park Avenue, which has disappeared.

Except for ground-floor "modernization," the exterior of the Gilsey House, now used for offices and light manufacturing, remains to a considerable degree as it was built more than a

century ago. Although it cost $300,000 to build, it became highly profitable when the theater district moved up to its part of Broadway.

The picture of the former luxury hotel, the Gilsey House, on p. 167 captures the modulating surface that is so different from the ultra-flat fronts of most iron stores and warehouses. Its baroque and undulating surface, especially along 29th St., is further emphasized by a recessed pavilion topped by a mansard tower with a curved roof. The tower is repeated on the Broadway facade and again further down 29th St. in a projecting portico. These pavilions are distinguised by flat pilasters bordering Palladian windows at every story. Flat marble areas along 29th St. separate narrower windows that have a hierarchy of pediments: urns and broken arches at the lower level, pediments at the next, segmental arches above and, finally, round-headed windows with keystones. The building's mansard roof is much less altered on the 29th St. side than on the Broadway front. In its heyday, the Gilsey House was painted a gleaming white.

Opposite is a detail photo of the three-story, curved crowning tower of the flamboyant mansard roof which signalized the grand front entrance to the hotel on the corner of Broadway and 29th St. Here the architect has piled one design element above another so that we see paired arched windows bearing a broken pediment from which peers a bull's-eye window that is topped by a triangular pediment. Teetering at this height is a great molded iron face which supports an elaborately framed clock.

The striking photograph of the 29th St. facade at the right helps us understand why—flamboyant, stylish and painted a pristine white—it attracted the coal magnates, railroad operators, congressmen and army and navy officers, who practically made it their headquarters. After it opened on April 15, 1871, the *New York Times* called it "one of the most imposing of our metropolitan palace hotels." A favorite spot was the bar, the floor of which was inlaid with silver dollars. The hotel later became a center for theater people, and it was here that the elder Oscar Hammerstein holed himself up when on a bet he wrote a three-act opera in 48 hours. The hotel closed on December 10, 1904.

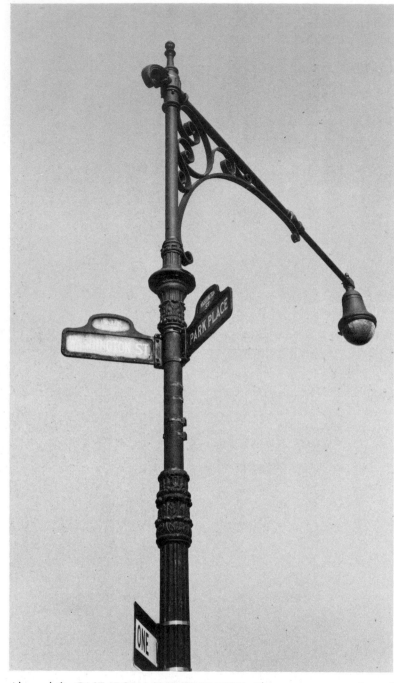

Above left: CAST-IRON LAMP POST (1892). This cross-arm version of the 1890s street light was devised to illuminate street intersections. The details of the design are very similar to those of the bishop's-crook lamp, except at the very top, where the pretty cast-iron leaf-and-vine scroll of the bishop's-crook lamp is replaced by a wrought-iron scrolled bracket holding the light itself well out over the roadway. From the street signs it can be seen that this lamp stands at the corner of Washington St. and Park Place in the heart of the old Washington Market section. This has been cleared in recent years and is known as the Washington Market Urban Renewal Area. The photo at the upper left, opposite, shows the base of the lamp with acanthus-leaf trim.

Above right: BISHOP'S-CROOK LAMPPOST (1900). A few of these beloved cast-iron lampposts are still to be found, left almost as if by mistake, on older streets. When electric lighting replaced the quite efficient gas lamps on New York streets, several companies supplied lighting in various sections of the city. According to passionate city-watcher Henry Hope Reed, all seem to have favored some version of this picturesque and practical iron post. It appears to have been copied from an English design still to be seen on the streets of such cities as Bristol and Bath. Martin Burrell, Head of New York's Department of Gas and Electricity, has arranged with the Friends of Cast-Iron Architecture to preserve *in situ* at least 30 of the old bishop's crook lamps as high-intensity lighting programs proceed.

Above right: GIBBES BUILDING, 66 WEST BROADWAY (detail). The Gibbes Building is a broad–fronted structure of shallow depth at the northwest corner of Murray St. The cast iron on its first and second floors is of unusual design, as can be seen in this photograph of the small–scale decoration appearing on six of its iron–clad piers. Its upper floors of tawny Roman brick have tall arches between giant pilasters. A person visiting the site should take a moment to observe an amusing anachronism pointed out by Alan Burnham of the Landmarks Commission. It is a sign on the building at the northwest corner of West Broadway and Warren St. which reads "College Place." This street name goes back to the time when Columbia College was located here.

Below right: 356 BROADWAY (detail). This picturesque cast–iron dormer window is set in a mansard roof with slates hung in an imbricated pattern. The roof ridge and cornice are pressed metal, while the four-story building itself is of masonry in a solid style with segmental arched windows and quoining at the sides. It was for decades the home of the House of Hadden & Co., "importers of raw silk and mattings." David Hadden founded the firm in 1806 at, of course, a location much farther downtown. The building is presently occupied by the Armed Forces Recruiting Center.

Above: 484 BROOME ST. (1890, Alfred Zucker; detail). One of the most sensational buildings in SoHo is a dark, honey–colored Romanesque extravaganza in sandstone and brick. It is to be seen at the northwest corner of Broome and Wooster Sts. Its broad window areas are made possible by the use of slender but powerful cast–iron supports. On the ground floor at four points the iron elements are marked by small applied cast–iron decorations that are utterly charming—twisted bundles of reeds and leaves tied in several places. We show one of these in our photograph.

Right: 427 BROADWAY (1870, Thomas R. Jackson; detail). This is one of the few columns that can be glimpsed on the ground floor of the beautiful cast–iron Dittenhofer Building. A tasteless remodeling of the first floor has hidden, or perhaps destroyed, most of the smooth–shafted columns, which, as in the picture here, have very unusual strap work enrichment on the lower portions. At the west end of the building's Howard St. facade, three or four of the original columns can be glimpsed, and, of course, the same style appears at the second story, where keystoned round arches spring from the Corinthian capitals. An intertwined, foliated design fills every spandrel and marks the frieze beneath the fine roof cornice, even embracing the numerals in the pediment. Each story is of decreasing height and is marked by a cornice. Surely, a harmony between horizontal and vertical is felt in this serene iron palazzo. Would that it could receive a fresh coat of paint! (Full description p. 135.)

172

Change: $14.00

All Sales Final
Thank you for supporting the Santa Fe
Animal Shelter and Humane Society

4912-43039

Invoice: 43039
Employee: Pam
December 1, 2015 15:39:04

ITEMS SOLD   Price

39UPQG	Paperback Books	1.00
39UPQG	Paperback Books	1.00
39UPQG	Paperback Books	1.00
39UPQG	Paperback Books	1.00
39UPQG	Paperback Books	1.00
39UPQG	Paperback Books	1.00

Sell Total:

Sub Total: $6.00

Total: $6.00

888 BROADWAY (1881, W. Wheeler Smith; details). A lissome palm frond spirals around a column that rests on a high pedestal which has a flower-and-leaf design in its panel—one of a row of exterior iron columns along the 19th St. side of this big corner building. Only the first floor is of cast iron; the upper floors are of tawny Haverford brick combined with terra-cotta. It was built as the great carpet emporium of W. & J. Sloane, which occupied it until 1912.

On the 19th St. side, the original first-floor design has not been enclosed to increase interior floor space, as it has along the Broadway frontage. Here we find the row of tall iron columns on high pedestals. Midway in the row stands the larger unique column with vining leaves and many-petalled flowers shown at the right. The upper part of the fluted shaft terminates in a capital with stylized leaves which cannot be seen in the picture.

Above left: 121 MERCER ST. (1879, David & John Jardine; detail). It has been said that more columns were cast in the iron foundries of New York than existed in the ancient world. Certainly the variety was incredible. A favorite treatment left the upper two thirds of the shaft plain, while the lowest third was decorated. Here the decoration consists of a heavy reeding topped by a band of stylized anthemion design. (Full description of building p. 85.)

Above right & right: 94 MERCER ST. (1884, Samuel A. Warner; detail). Idealized iron flowers appear as decoration on each of 14 tall pillars on the first floor of a brick building on the east side of Mercer St. just south of Spring St. The pictures of two examples of the flower decoration show one flower intact, the other partially cracked away and disclosing the character of the heavy iron pier behind it. They also demonstrate the involved craftsmanship and the many individual castings that were combined to create the cast–iron architecture of even the rear of a commercial building. The Mercer St. elevation is the back of a truly impressive structure on the west side of Broadway built in 1884 to designs by Samuel A. Warner. The Broadway facade, which is in the so-called Queen Anne style, combines with verve red brick, sculptured red terra–cotta and ironwork. Covering the lots of 515–517–519 Broadway, the building stands on part of the site of the fabulous mid–19th–century St. Nicholas Hotel.

Left: 127–131 MERCER ST. (1881). A six-story gray brick building of some pretensions has on its ground floor flat cast-iron pilasters. These bear a guilloche-type design placed in depressed panels above and below a stylized rosette in a roundel. Painted green, the pilasters flank a pedimented doorway where cast iron again is used. The door and its surround are painted a bright fireman's red. Is this not to remind us that an old volunteer firehouse, the famous Second Fireman's Hall built in 1830, once occupied part of the site? The Third Fireman's Hall is still in use at 155 Mercer St. Now 127 Mercer houses a wool stock company, while artists are ensconced on some of the upper floors. A large gas-light fixture factory was once located here.

Above: 362 WEST BROADWAY (detail). This photograph, capturing the first-floor details of two adjacent buildings, is a testament to the variety and skill of the iron caster's art. For contrasts in style, you can't beat the SoHo cast-iron district. The Landmarks Commission has designated it—quite properly all 25 blocks of it—a Historic District.

Above & above left: GRACE CHURCH, BROADWAY AT 10 ST. (1846, James Renwick, Jr.; details). This charming gothic cast-iron fence surrounds the grassy grounds of the church house and rectory of famous old Grace Protestant Episcopal Church on the eastern edge of Greenwich Village. According to the rector, Dr. Benjamin Minifie, it is safe to assume that the fence was put up when the buildings were completed inasmuch as it appears in the earliest pictures depicting them. The gate carries a quaint cast-iron address plaque which says "802, Sexton's Office, Grace House."

Below left: U.S. ARMY BUILDING, WHITEHALL ST. (1886; detail). A patriotic iron fence, part wrought iron, part cast iron, surrounds the old Army Building on Whitehall St. between Water and Pearl Sts. This typical section of the fence shows the cast-iron shields bearing the proper number of stripes and stars for 1888, when it was made, and the cast-iron fence posts which are topped by cannon balls below which appears on each post a star in a sunken circular panel.

DAKOTA APARTMENTS, 1 WEST 72 ST. (1884, Henry J. Hardenbergh). For sheer snap, there is no ornamental ironwork in the city to compare with the boldly conceived fence surrounding the monumental Dakota Apartments, 72nd St. and Central Park West. Repeated many times in the long fence, which borders a moat, this image of a fierce old man and his fantastic attendants is a product of the high art of 19th-century iron casting. The Hecla Iron Works displayed a similar section of the fence at the front of their showroom, for clearly it was a sample of their work in which they took great pride. The 1884 Dakota, the city's first luxury apartments, was the German Renaissance design of architect Henry J. Hardenbergh, built in what was at the time a remote section of the city for an expensive residential structure. This fact explains its names, which was derived from the joking remark that it was as far away as the Dakotas. It is a designated city landmark.

Above: ARSENAL, 830 FIFTH AVENUE (1847, Martin E. Thompson). The arsenal on the eastern margin of Central Park, Fifth Avenue and 64th St., stood here before there was a park or even much of a Fifth Avenue. Built in 1847–48 as a New York State arsenal, its purpose was military. A mere 10 years later the state agreed to sell it and its grounds to the city for $275,000 for incorporation in the new park then being created. In their Greensward Plan for the new park, Olmsted and Vaux proposed that the arsenal be used as a museum, and so it was for the years 1869 to 1877, while the Museum of Natural History used the top floor. Later the arsenal became the permanent home of the Parks Department and now it is headquarters for the Parks, Recreation and Cultural Affairs Administration. It is a designated landmark. The cast-iron decoration on the building's main entrance is notable. For one thing, the handrail up either side of the steep flight of steps is supported on 10 cast-iron rifles stood on end. The iron doors at the entry way are framed by sunken iron panels with designs of weapons in sharp relief—spears, halberds and crossed swords—while across the top of the doors is a vigilant eagle, beak open, wings spread. On either side of him are pyramidal piles of cannonballs. Crenellations over his head suggest a fortification. No one seems to know who created this bold public sculpture in iron.

Right: 101 SPRING ST. (1870, Nicholas Whyte; detail). Detail of the iron decoration on the ground floor. No Renaissance inspiration here. Three clustered slender columns, concealing the supporting pier, rest lightly on this sturdy base with mechanistic trim. Note that the iron has been chipped away, probably by a truck. (Full description of building p. 57.)

Left: OLD B. ALTMAN STORE, SIXTH AVENUE AT 19 ST. (1876, David & John Jardine; detail). Only these strong square decorated iron columns remain on the otherwise bastardized ground floor of what was once the elegant B. Altman's department store. Architects David and John Jardine gave Neo-Grec embellishment to their stylish 1876 iron front. Here the iron cladding of an inner structural corner pier displays delicately incised flat surfaces above a modeled base. (Full description p. 105.)

Above: FIRST PRESBYTERIAN CHURCH, FIFTH AVENUE AT 11 ST. (1845, Joseph C. Wells; detail). The date and architect's name listed here apply to the dignified brownstone church on lower Fifth Avenue, but not to its fence, of which we show a photograph. The iron fence, at least the part of it along the Fifth Avenue side of the church grounds, is much older than the church. It was brought up from Wall St., where a Presbyterian church had been located from 1720. A new church was erected on the Wall St. site in 1811, and at some point in its history this fence was set up around it. That church had a serious fire in 1834, and although it was rebuilt in the next few months, the congregation decided to build this new church uptown north of Washington Square.

74 GRAND ST. (1876, George da Cunha). This is a very typical 19th-century cast-iron warehouse front door with its several steps, the top one providing for convenient loading into the back of a horse-drawn wagon. Today's trucks, backing up to such loading steps, often deal murderous blows to cast-iron elements, cracking them apart, even knocking off entire sections. In this picture it can be seen that a careful owner has used sheet metal to patch the base of the center column.

CHELSEA HOTEL, 222 WEST 23 ST. (1883, Hubert, Pirrson & Co; detail). The Chelsea Hotel, known the world round for its artistic and Bohemian clientele, is also noteworthy for its exquisite decorative cast iron—so beautiful it stays in the memory after a single glimpse. In the entire city there is nothing to compare with the strip balconies, which, like long lengths of iron lace, enhance the massive brick facade. A repeated design of interlaced sunflowers and leaves suggests Art Nouveau but stops short of its languid, flowing grace and is more properly regarded as in the Queen Anne style. These balconies were fabricated by the great Cornell foundry, which by this time was under the direction of J. B. Cornell and his son J. M. Cornell. The ground floor incorporates a good deal of monumental ironwork vaguely Gothic in inspiration. To judge by a label near the front entrance, this iron was cast in the Z. S. Ayres Iron Foundry. The lobby, which had become a drab vestibule, has been transformed, through a felicitous collaboration of management and gifted residents, into a brightly colored art gallery, its walls hung with colorful paintings by its present or recent tenants.

What was once its most dramatic feature, the cast-iron staircase which spirals up to a top-floor skylight, has been enclosed to comply with fire laws. However, it is still there behind doors and can be viewed by anyone willing to climb two flights. Its ironwork also incorporates a flower motif. It is said that the Chelsea was built as a 12-story cooperative apartment house and had the first penthouse in New York City. Its dull red brick walls, described as three feet thick, with even the partitions between the rooms of solid brick, make the hotel virtually soundproof, so that practicing musicians disturb no one. Virgil Thomson composed two operas here. The hotel has harbored innumerable other artists and writers, among them John Sloan, who had a cluttered old duplex apartment in it. A few of the many notable writers were O. Henry, Thomas Wolfe, Dylan Thomas, Brendan Behan and Tennessee Williams. Mark Twain stayed here during a lecture tour, and Sarah Bernhardt, who is said to have adored the hotel, lived here while playing at the Booth Theater a block away. Lillian Russell lived at the Chelsea through her entire run of 33 weeks at Procter's 23rd Street Theater.

Top: TRADEMARK OF ARCHITECTURAL IRON WORKS. This trademark or label of the celebrated Architectural Iron Works is to be found on many of the important iron-front buildings of the 1850s and 1860s in New York, including a number shown in the present book. The firm's large illustrated catalogue, which the proprietor, Daniel D. Badger, issued in 1865, has been reprinted by Da Capo. It is a boon to anyone doing serious study of the uniquely American iron buildings. One of the largest manufacturers of these in the entire country, Badger's Architectural Iron Works was on the corner of Avenue C and 14th St. near the present Stuyvesant Town. The office was at 42 Duane.

Bottom: TRADEMARK OF CORNELL IRON WORKS. John B. Cornell and his brother William W. went into the iron business when architectural ironwork was in its infancy. Theirs became one of the largest foundries in the city, starting at 141 Centre St. south of Canal St. and eventually adding a second large foundry and fitting shops covering 70 city lots on West 26th St. along the Hudson River. This firm manufactured the iron parts for several of the buildings included in this book. Inasmuch as William W. Cornell died in 1870, any building bearing a label with his initials, such as that shown in the photograph, was erected before 1871. Later labels bear the initials of the father, J. B., with those of his son, J. M. Such labels can be found, for example, at 648 Broadway and 550 Broadway. J. B. Cornell's home at the northwest corner of Fifth Avenue and 44th St. became the Fifth Avenue Bank, which was demolished within only the last few years. The Cornell Iron Works is still in business, specializing in their rolling metal shutters and folding metal doors, under the management of the Cornell family.

Index of
CAST-IRON BUILDINGS

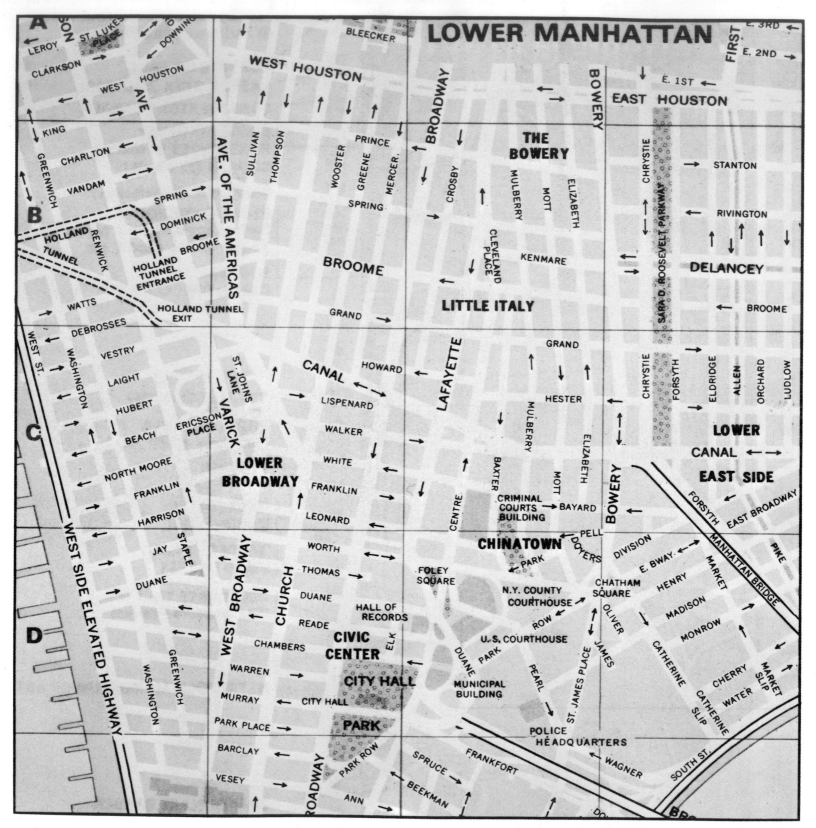

LOWER MANHATTAN

Reproduced with permission from *New York in Flashmaps*
by Toy Lasker. Copyright © 1974 by Flashmaps, Inc.